Language Essentials for Teachers of Reading and Spelling

LETRS

Module 1

The Challenge of Learning to Read

Second Edition

Louisa C. Moats, Ed.D.

Carol Tolman, Ed.D.

Presenter's Kit by Carol Tolman

Sopris West®
EDUCATIONAL SERVICES

A Cambium Learning® Company

BOSTON, MA · LONGMONT, CO

Printed in the United States of America
Published and Distributed by

Sopris West®
EDUCATIONAL SERVICES

A Cambium Learning® Company
17855 Dallas Parkway, Suite 400 • Dallas, TX 75287
800.547.6747 • www.voyagersoprislearning.com

How does copyright pertain to LETRS® Module 1?

- It is illegal to reproduce any part of the LETRS Module 1 book in any way and for any reason without written permission from the copyright holder, Sopris West® Educational Services. This applies to copying, scanning, retyping, etc.
- It is illegal to reproduce LETRS Module 1 materials to distribute or present at a workshop without written permission from the copyright holder.
- It is illegal to use the name LETRS in association with any workshop, materials, training, publications, etc., without written permission from the copyright holder.

Dedication

To my husband, Steve Mitchell, who publishes, supports, and believes in our work.

—LCM

To Scot, Michaela, and Keagan, who are my world.

… and to Louisa Moats. I do not take lightly the fact that I am coauthoring this edition of LETRS® with Louisa. I am humbled and honored to be but a small part of this incredible endeavor, one that has taught me as much as I have taught others.

—CT

Acknowledgments

LETRS® modules have been developed with the help of many people. The national LETRS trainers—including Mary Dahlgren, Nancy Hennessy, Susan Hall, Marcia Davidson, Deb Glaser, Linda Farrell, Judi Dodson, Pat Sekel, Joan Sedita, Anthony Fierro, and Anne Whitney—have offered valuable suggestions for improving module content and structure. Their commitment to delivering LETRS across the country is appreciated beyond measure.

Bruce Rosow, Kevin Feldman, Susan Lowell, Patricia Mathes, Marianne Steverson, Lynn Kuhn, Jan Hasbrouck, Marsha Berger, Susan Smartt, and Nancy Eberhardt contributed their expertise to all LETRS first edition modules and often provide valuable input and feedback. Many other professionals from all over the country who have attended institutes and offered constructive criticism have enabled the continual improvement of LETRS and related materials. We hope you see your influence on all of the second edition modules.

We are grateful for the competent support of the Sopris West editorial and production staff, including Holly Bell, Jeff Dieffenbach, Michelle LaBorde, Rob Carson, Karen Butler, Sherri Rowe, Geoff Horsfall, Jill Stanko, and Kay Power. Special thanks are due to Toni Backstrom, who manages the LETRS program with enthusiasm, competence, and flare, and to Steve Mitchell, the publisher of LETRS.

About the Authors

Louisa C. Moats, Ed.D., is a nationally recognized authority on reading instruction, how children learn to read, why many people have trouble reading, and treatment of reading problems. Louisa has been a neuropsychology technician, teacher, graduate school instructor, licensed psychologist, researcher, conference speaker, and author. She spent 15 years in private practice in Vermont, specializing in evaluation of and consultation with individuals of all ages who experienced difficulty with reading, spelling, writing, and oral language. After advising the California Reading Initiative for one year, Louisa was site director of the NICHD Early Interventions Project in Washington, D.C., a four-year project that included daily work with inner-city teachers and children. Recently, she has devoted herself to the improvement of teacher training and professional development.

Louisa earned her bachelor's degree at Wellesley College, her master's degree at Peabody College of Vanderbilt, and her doctorate in reading and human development from the Harvard Graduate School of Education. She was licensed to teach in three states before undertaking her doctoral work. In addition to LETRS®, Louisa has authored and coauthored books including *Speech to Print: Language Essentials for Teachers; Spelling: Development, Disability, and Instruction; Straight Talk About Reading* (with Susan Hall), *Parenting a Struggling Reader* (with Susan Hall), and *Basic Facts About Dyslexia and Other Reading Problems* (with Karen Dakin). Instructional materials include *Spellography* (with Bruce Rosow) and *Spelling by Pattern* (with Ellen Javernick and Betty Hooper).

Louisa's many journal articles, book chapters, and policy papers include the American Federation of Teachers' *Teaching Reading Is Rocket Science*, the Learning First Alliance's *Every Child Reading: A Professional Development Guide*, and Reading First's *Blueprint for Professional Development*.

Carol Tolman, Ed.D., is a leading national LETRS® trainer who has taught LETRS modules in the states of Montana, Iowa, Delaware, Texas, Colorado, and Louisiana. Carol comes to both LETRS and DIBELS® training with 25 years of classroom and clinical teaching experience in public schools. She spent 12 of those years designing and implementing an innovative, exemplary program for academically challenged high school students.

Carol is the author of the International Dyslexia Association's (IDA) *Perspectives* article "Working Harder, Not Smarter: What Teachers of Reading Need to Know and Be Able to Teach." She is lead author of LETRS *Presenter's Kits* as well as coauthor of *The Reading Coach: Presenter's Kit* (with Jan Hasbrouck and Carolyn Denton). Carol's credentials include a master's degree in curriculum and instruction, and a doctorate in educational psychology with a concentration in reading from American International College.

Contents

Introduction to LETRS® 1
Content of LETRS Modules Within the Language-Literacy Connection 3
Overview of Module 1 3

Chapter 1 Why Reading Instruction Is a National Priority
Learner Objective for Chapter 1 5
Warm-Up Questions 5
Reading Problems Are Common 5
Instruction Matters 6

Chapter 2 Learning to Read Is Not Natural
Learner Objectives for Chapter 2 7
Warm-Up: Listening to Forms of Language 7
Speaking Is Natural; Reading and Writing Are Not 8
Table 2.1: Progression of Typical Oral Language Development 8
Language and Literacy 9
Spoken and Written Language Differ 10
Exercise 2.1: Comparing Spoken and Written Language 11
What Is Special About an Alphabet? 13
Figure 2.1: Flowchart of the Evolution of Alphabetic Writing 15
Awareness of Speech Sounds and the Alphabetic Principle 16
Figure 2.2: Types of Writing Systems 16
Shallow and Deep Orthographies 16
Advantages of an Alphabetic System 18
Exercise 2.2: Simulation of Learning to Read 23
Take 2 Review 27

Chapter 3 What the Brain Does When It Reads
Learner Objectives for Chapter 3 29
Warm-Up: Watch Eye Movements 29
Eye Movements and Reading 29
Figure 3.1: What the Eye Takes in During Fixations 30
Proficient Reading Depends on Many Skills 31
Figure 3.2: Two Domains and Five Essential Components of Reading 31
Four Processing Systems That Support Word Recognition 32
Areas of the Brain Involved in Reading 32
Figure 3.3: Areas of the Brain That Support Reading 32
Jobs of the Four Processing Systems 33
Figure 3.4: The Four-Part Processing Model for Word Recognition 33
Exercise 3.1: Acting Out the Brain 34
The Job of the Phonological Processor 34
The Job of the Orthographic Processor 35

The Job of the Meaning Processor 36
The Job of the Context Processor. 36
Exercise 3.2: The Four Processors at Work in the Classroom 37
Alternative Exercise 3.2: Processing Systems and Classroom Instruction 38
Moving Beyond Cueing Systems 39
Take 2 Review 40

Chapter 4 How Children Learn to Read and Spell

Learner Objectives for Chapter 4 41
Warm-Up: Look Closely at Spelling. 41
The Continuum of Reading and Spelling Development 42
The Developing Reading Brain. 42
Figure 4.1: Reading Levels and Reliance on Different Regions of the Brain 42
The Connecticut Longitudinal Study 43
Table 4.1: How the Relationship Between Decoding and Comprehension
Changes Over Time 43
Chall's Pioneering Description of Reading "Stages" 44
Ehri's Model of Reading Progression 45
Figure 4.2: Ehri's Phases of Word-Reading Development. 45
Table 4.2: Phases of Reading and Spelling Development 46
Case Study Examples of Early Reading and Spelling Development 47
Prealphabetic Reading and Spelling 47
Figure 4.3: Prealphabetic Writing 47
Early Alphabetic Reading and Spelling 48
Figure 4.4: Early Alphabetic Writing 48
Exercise 4.1: Sounds in Letter Names 49
Later Alphabetic Reading and Spelling 50
Figure 4.5: Later Alphabetic Writing. 50
Consolidated Alphabetic Stage 51
Brain Studies of Reading Growth. 51
Figure 4.6: How Activation Patterns in the Brain Change as Reading Is Learned . . . 52
Achieving Passage-Reading Fluency With Comprehension. 53
Scarborough's "Rope" Model of Reading Development 54
Figure 4.7: The Many Strands That Are Woven Into Skilled Reading 54
Exercise 4.2: Review Reading and Spelling Development With Writing Samples . . . 55
Alternative Exercise 4.2: For Teachers of Older Students 56
Five Essential Components of Comprehensive Reading Instruction 57
Where did the five essential components come from? 57
What should be emphasized at each stage of reading development? 57
Table 4.3: Reading Instruction Components Typically Emphasized at
Each Grade Level 58

Chapter 5 Dyslexia and Other Causes of Reading Disability

Learner Objectives for Chapter 5 59
Warm-Up: Identify a Student With Reading Difficulties 59
Reading Problems Have Many Causes 59

What Is Dyslexia? 59
Subtypes of Reading Disability 60
    Figure 5.1: Diagram of Subtypes of Reading Disability. 60
The Brain and Dyslexia. 62
    Figure 5.2: Brain Images Comparing 9-Year-Old Average Reader and 9-Year-Old
    Unremediated Poor Reader 62
    Figure 5.3: Changes in Brain Activation Patterns in Response to Instruction 63
    The School History of the Dyslexic Person 63
    Exercise 5.1: Three Second-Grade Children With Three Kinds of Reading Problems . 66
Implications for Assessment 69
    Exercise 5.2: DIBELS and the Four Processors 70
    Take 2 Review 71

Chapter 6 The Research Base for Understanding Reading

    Learner Objectives for Chapter 6 73
    Warm-Up: List Your Favorite Resources. 73
Why Bother With Scientific Research? 73
    What Is Scientific Research? 74
        Exercise 6.1: Qualitative and Quantitative Research 75
        Exercise 6.2: Understanding Effect Size 78
        Figure 6.1: Normal Curve With Standard Deviations and Percentages 78
        Exercise 6.3: Shared Reading of a Research Article 79
        Exercise 6.4: Module 1 Review: Match It! 81

Chapter 7 Leadership to Improve Reading and Language Skills

    Learner Objectives for Chapter 7 83
    Warm-Up 83
What Successful Schools Do 83
    The Purpose of Leadership 84
    A Reality: Reading Problems Are Resistant to Change. 84
    Data Utilization and Analysis 85
    Response to Intervention (RtI) and Tiered Instructional Models 86
    Scientifically Based Classroom Programs. 87
    The Use of Supplementary Programs and Materials 88
    Intensive Intervention for Students With Severe Reading Disabilities 88
    Beyond Grade 3: Teaching Older, Poor Readers 89
    Professional Development for Teachers 89
        Exercise 7.1: Action Plan for Principals 91
Final Review, Module 1 93

xiv Contents

Appendix A: Instructor Script for *Exercise 2.2:* Simulation of Learning to Read 95

Appendix B: Colorado Teacher Preparation Program Criteria for Literacy Courses. 105

Appendix C: Extension Activities 111

Glossary 113

Bibliography 119

Answer Key 127

Index 143

Introduction to LETRS®

LETRS® (*Language Essentials for Teachers of Reading and Spelling*) is professional development for educators who are responsible for improving K–12 instruction in reading, writing, and spelling. The content of LETRS is delivered in a series of 12 core modules in book format. Each module in the series focuses on one topic, with the topics aligned to be delivered in sequential training. Thus, one book for use in the course of training—and later as a professional reference—is provided for each module. Each module is typically delivered in a one- to two-day presentation by a national, regional, or local district trainer who has met the LETRS trainer certification guidelines developed by Dr. Moats and her colleagues.

module [mŏjūl] n.

a self-contained component of a whole that is used in conjunction with, and has a well-defined connection to, the other components

LETRS modules are used for both in-service training and for undergraduate and graduate courses in reading and literacy. They can also be resources for any educator charged with improving the language skills of students. LETRS is designed so that participants will understand:

1. *How* children learn to read and *why* some children have difficulty with this aspect of literacy;
2. *What* must be taught during reading and spelling lessons and *how to teach* most effectively;
3. *Why* all components of reading instruction are necessary and *how* they are related;
4. *How to interpret* individual differences in student achievement; and
5. *How to explain* the form and structure of English.

LETRS modules are designed to be delivered in sequence, but flexible sequencing is possible. In sequence, the modules build on overview concepts and introductory content, and then on phonology, phoneme awareness, and the writing system (orthography) of English (Modules 1–3). Next, the modules progress to topics in vocabulary, fluency, and comprehension instruction (Modules 4–6). Later modules (7–9) target reading instruction for the primary grades and include a module on assessment for prevention and early intervention. The final series (Modules 10–12), designed for educators who work with students at grade 3 and above, address advanced phonics and word study, comprehension and study skills in content-area reading, and assessment.

A presenter CD-ROM (developed by Dr. Carol Tolman) accompanies each LETRS module, providing a PowerPoint® presentation that supports, extends, and elaborates module content. The presentation slides are designed to be used by professional development personnel, higher education faculty, consultants, reading specialists, and coaches who have a strong background in the concepts and who have been trained to deliver LETRS modules.

LETRS is not a reading instruction program, and LETRS modules do not substitute for program-specific training. Rather, LETRS complements and supports the implementation of programs aligned with scientifically based reading research (SBRR). A complete approach to improving reading instruction must include: (a) selection and use of core and supplemental instructional materials; (b) professional development on how to use the materials; (c) professional development that leads to broader understandings; (d) classroom coaching and in-school supports; (e) an assessment program for data-based problem-solving; and (f) strong leadership. A comprehensive, systemic approach with these elements will support a Response to Intervention (RtI) initiative.

We recommend that teachers who have had little experience with or exposure to the science of reading and research-based practices begin with LETRS *Foundations* (Glaser & Moats, 2008). *Foundations* is a stepping stone into the regular LETRS modules. Other related resources have been developed to support LETRS professional development, including:

- LETRS Interactive CD-ROMs for Modules 2, 3, 4, 7, and 8 (developed with a grant from the Small Business Innovation Research [SBIR] program of the National Institute of Child Health and Human Development [NICHD]), which provide additional content and skill practice for topics often considered challenging to implement and teach in the classroom.
- *ParaReading: A Training Guide for Tutors* (Glaser, 2005)
- *The Reading Coach* (Hasbrouck & Denton, 2005)
- *Teaching English Language Learners: A Supplementary* LETRS *Module* (Arguelles & Baker, in press)
- *Early Childhood* LETRS (Hart Paulson, in press)
- *Teaching Reading Essentials* (Moats & Farrell, 2007), a series of video modeling used extensively by LETRS trainers throughout the delivery of training.

The chart on the next page represents a fundamental idea in LETRS—that language systems underlie reading and writing, and students' difficulties with reading and writing are most effectively addressed if the structures and functions of language are taught to them directly. We ask teachers to learn the terminology of language systems and to recognize that language is an important common denominator that links reading with writing, speaking, and listening comprehension.

Content of LETRS Modules Within the Language-Literacy Connection

Components of Comprehensive Reading Instruction	Organization of Language						
	Phonology	Morphology	Orthography	Semantics	Syntax	Discourse and Pragmatics	Etymology
Phonological Awareness	2	2					
Phonics, Spelling, and Word Study	3, 7	3, 7, 10	3, 7, 10				3, 10
Fluency	5	5	5	5	5		
Vocabulary	4	4	4	4	4		4
Text Comprehension		6		6	6	6, 11	
Written Expression			9, 11	9, 11	9, 11	9, 11	
Assessment	8, 12	8, 12	8, 12	8, 12	8, 12	8, 12	

Note: Numbers represent individual modules in the LETRS series.

Overview of Module 1

Module 1 introduces participants to the five essential components of instruction but emphasizes the language skills that link those components and the relationships among word recognition, fluency, and comprehension. This module:

- teaches concepts and frameworks for understanding how children learn to read;
- explains why some children have difficulty with the reading aspect of literacy;
- presents the implications of the differences between spoken and written language;
- teaches a scientifically validated framework for understanding reading development that is used in subsequent modules for interpretation of student work samples and test results;
- defines and describes dyslexia, along with other validated subtypes of reading difficulties; and
- includes optional sections on understanding scientifically based reading research and on leadership for implementing a reading initiative.

Module 1 includes many activities that require participants to move, talk, think, and respond. Chapters are organized around explicit objectives that are taught, practiced, and targeted in exercises and a final module review. Concepts introduced in Module 1 are revisited, reinforced, and applied in later modules.

Chapter 1

Why Reading Instruction Is a National Priority

Learner Objective for Chapter 1

- Survey the evidence that reading problems are common.

Warm-Up Questions

As your instructor poses each question, briefly relate your answers to a partner:

1. Approximately how many students in your school, district, or state are viewed as poor readers at the end of grade 3?_____

2. By what criteria are those students identified (e.g., state end-of-grade test, benchmarks on screening measures, NAEP scores)?_____

   _____

3. Are your local school statistics better than, the same as, or worse than state averages?

   _____

4. Are you satisfied with your class's achievement in reading, spelling, writing, and/or language? _____

Reading Problems Are Common

National concern about the quality of our schools and the achievement of all students is higher than it has ever been. Throughout the 1990s, the National Institute of Child Health and Human Development (NICHD) characterized reading difficulty as a major public health concern that deserved high priority on the national research agenda (Sweet, 2004). The inability to read well is associated with social ills such as dropping out of school, delinquency, inadequate health care, unwanted pregnancy, and chronic underemployment. According to the most recent National Assessment of Educational Progress (National Center for Education Statistics [NCES], 2005), inadequate reading skills are characteristic of approximately 38 percent of fourth-grade students nationally and up to 70 percent of poor students, especially African American, Hispanic, and Native American children who live in urban or isolated

NAPE website

5

areas. Unless children learn to read well, they will be significantly disadvantaged in 21st century society. These facts led Congress to steadily increase the proportion of our national health research dollars allotted to reading research to create the National Reading Panel (National Institute of Child Health & Human Development [NICHD], 2000) to fund the Reading First program within the No Child Left Behind Act of 2001, and to fund research through the Institute of Education Sciences in the U.S. Department of Education.

Instruction Matters

The devastating educational and social consequences of reading failure can often be prevented (Fletcher, Lyon, Fuchs & Barnes, 2007; Foorman, 2003; Torgesen, 2002). Studies that emphasize both classroom instruction and supplemental intervention programs have found that all but 2–5 percent of children can learn basic reading skills in first grade, even in populations where the incidence of poor reading is very high (Mathes et al., 2005). In addition, higher levels of literacy are possible when students achieve basic reading skills early in their school careers (Cunningham & Stanovich, 1998; Foorman, Francis, Shaywitz, Shaywitz, & Fletcher, 1997). Older students with reading problems can also improve to grade level if their remediation is sufficiently intensive, expert, and long-term (Torgesen, Alexander, et al., 2001).

Student success, however, depends on whether teachers use sound, proven, effective programs and practices, and whether those practices are implemented with sufficient skill and intensity. This module of LETRS presents major conceptual frameworks that are derived from research across many scientific disciplines that should inform our practices. Best practices described by research may be embodied in published programs of instruction, but informed teachers are the best assurance that those practices will be sustained. Programs don't teach; teachers do.

We begin with consideration of what reading requires of the learner, how language and reading are related, how the nature of reading changes over time, and what goes wrong when students have difficulty.

2 Learning to Read Is Not Natural

Learner Objectives for Chapter 2
- Examine the ways that spoken and written language differ.
- Explain the special characteristics of "academic language."
- Contrast alphabetic writing with non-alphabetic writing.
- Experience "learning to read" with novel symbols.

Warm-Up: Listening to Forms of Language
1. First, listen to or role-play a typical cell phone conversation.
2. Next, listen to the following passages as your instructor reads them aloud.

> **Narrative text** (from *Stuart Little*; White, 2005):
> Stuart peered ahead into the gathering storm, but saw nothing except gray waves with white crests. The world seemed cold and ominous. Stuart glanced behind him. There came the sloop, boiling along fast, rolling up a bow wave and gaining steadily.
> "Look out, Stuart! Look out where you're going!"
> Stuart strained his eyes and suddenly, dead ahead, right in the path of the Wasp, he saw an enormous paper bag looming up on the surface of the pond. The bag was empty and riding high, its open end gaping wide like the mouth of a cave …
>
> **Expository text** (from *World of Baby Animals*; Hodgson, 1995):
> … Among canine predators, puppies get an early start. Adult wolves will playfully ambush youngsters, and then allow them to tag along on hunts at three months of age. Occasionally an adult will step on a pup and hold it down, a playful gesture which biologists feel may duplicate that used by adult males and females to affirm rank within the pack.

3. What are some obvious ways that these passages differ from a cell phone conversation?

Speaking Is Natural; Reading and Writing Are Not

Spoken language is "hard–wired" inside the human brain. Language capacity in humans evolved about 100,000 years ago, and the human brain is fully adapted for language processing. Any child, unless neurologically impaired or hearing impaired, will learn to talk. By the time a child is 10 months of age, he or she has already learned how to recognize the speech sounds (or phonemes) of the language spoken by caregivers (see *Table 2.1*). At the same time, the child has lost some of the capacity to distinguish and produce the phonemes of other languages (Kuhl, Williams, Lacerda, Stevens, & Lindblom, 1992).

Even 1-year-olds comprehend much of what is said by others. Most children generate simple sentences by the time they are 16 to 24 months of age. The few children known to scientists who did not learn to speak in early childhood, such as the French "Wild Boy of Aveyron" and the closet child, Genie (Curtis, 1977),[1] were almost totally isolated from other people during their critical early years.

Table 2.1 Progression of Typical Oral Language Development

(from American Speech-Language-Hearing Association [ASHA] Web site: http://www.asha.org/public/speech/development/01.htm)

0–3 months	4–6 months	7 months– 1 year	1–2 years	2–3 years	3–4 years	4–5 years
Coos, cries, smiles	Babbles are more speech-like, includes many sounds such as /p/, /b/, /m/	Imitates different speech sounds, longer groups of sounds, begins saying words such as **bye-bye**, **mama**, **dada**	Uses more words each month, puts two words together into phrases, asks questions like "Where kitty?"	Has words for almost everything, uses two to three words together, is more easily understood, especially by those who know child	Says sentences with four or more words, talks about activities and/or people, is easily understood by all	Uses clear voice, detailed sentences, sticks to topic, uses appropriate grammar, says most sounds correctly

A related fact should be self-evident: Reading and writing are acquired skills for which the human brain is not yet fully evolved (Liberman, Shankweiler, & Liberman, 1989). Human brains are naturally wired to speak; they are not naturally wired to read and write. With teaching, children typically learn to read at about age 5 or 6 and need several years to master the skill. Sophisticated reading comprehension is the goal of 8 to 16 more years of schooling.

---

[1]   Curtis, S. (1977). *Genie: A linguistic study of a modern-day "wild child."* New York: Academic Press. Also, the Francois Truffaut film, *The Wild Child*, depicts the case of Victor, an abandoned child discovered in the woods and brought to an asylum in France in 1798. The film was written about in Roger Shattuck's (1980) *The Forbidden Experiment: The Story of the Wild Boy of Aveyron.*

Thus, for most students, reading and writing need to be directly taught!

In the United States, the federal government estimates that 14 percent of the adult population is "below basic" and unable to perform functional reading tasks (National Adult Literacy Survey, 2003). Another 29 percent are "at basic" but below "intermediate." Only 13 percent are classified as "proficient." The two lowest groups do not read with the fluency, accuracy, and comprehension necessary to decipher newspapers, health guidelines, schedules, or manuals. Although adults are constantly exposed to print in the environment, they may not learn to read. The myth (perpetuated as fact) that people learn to read naturally just by being immersed in print results in misguided instructional practices. Traces of the "natural" theory of reading acquisition continue to be visible in many publications and programs (Moats, 2000, 2006). However, current information about the prevalence, causes, and remedies for reading difficulty indicates beyond doubt that reading, spelling, writing, and language mastery are challenging for a substantial proportion of the U.S. population, and many students are dependent on systematic, direct teaching to become literate.

> ## Teaching Tips
>
> **What can you do?**
> - Read your students' files. Interview parents to find instances of late oral language development.
> - Identify potential red flags for literacy issues:
>   - Ear infections?
>   - Tubes in ears, delayed speech noted, illnesses, infections, etc.?
>   - Family history of speech difficulties?
>   - Receiving speech services?
>   - English as a Second Language (ELL/ESL)?
>
> **Oral language is a foundational skill for reading and writing.**

Language and Literacy

Language proficiency and reading, spelling, and writing achievement are strongly related to one another. A recent study of 1,350 children in 127 urban classrooms in grades 1–4 (Mehta, Foorman, Branum-Martin, & Taylor, 2005) examined the extent to which word-reading, spelling, and comprehension are related to one another and general language competence. The study also examined how teacher effectiveness and students' beginning skill levels predicted growth in reading achievement over the first four years of schooling. The results illustrated that literacy achievement and language levels were very closely correlated in these classrooms. Word-reading accuracy and fluency were shown to be very important factors in reading comprehension in the early grades. The literacy achievement levels of first- to fourth-grade classrooms, however, were perfectly predicted by the composite vocabulary and language proficiency scores of each classroom.

Visual perception, visual-motor skills, and visual-spatial reasoning (e.g., puzzle construction, the ability to draw) are surprisingly unrelated to reading and writing skill (Vellutino, Tunmer, Jaccard, & Chen, 2007). People who are very good in art, mechanics, dance, acting, or navigation may not be good at reading, spelling, writing, or using language. When individuals have nonverbal talents in the arts, spatial/mechanical reasoning, or athletics, those strengths may enable them to cope with reading or language difficulties, but they will still require explicit teaching of reading and language skills in order to become literate.

Given the importance of language to literacy, our approach to understanding reading and writing will frequently reference the structures of language. The structures, or systems, of language that will be explored throughout LETRS include:

Language System	Definition	Example
phonology	The rule system within a language by which phonemes can be sequenced, combined, and pronounced to make words	No English word begins with the sound /ng/; the sounds /p/ and /k/ are never adjacent in the same syllable.
orthography	A writing system for representing language	Every English word ending in /v/ is spelled with **-ve**.
morphology	The study of meaningful units in a language and how the units are combined in word formation	*Nat-* is a root. **Nature** is a noun; **natural** is an adjective; **naturalist** is a noun; **naturally** is an adverb.
semantics	The study of word and phrase meanings and relationships	The word **rank** has multiple meanings. The words **order** and **sequence** have similar meanings.
syntax	The system of rules governing permissible word order in sentences	"Our district recruits new teachers" is a sentence; "New teachers our district recruits" is not a sentence.
discourse	Organizational conventions in longer segments of oral or written language	Paragraph structure; cohesive ties; genre conventions such as story structure
pragmatics	The system of rules and conventions for using language and related gestures in a social context	To one person I say, "That is my seat!" To another, I say, "Excuse me, my ticket has that seat number."

Spoken and Written Language Differ

© Cartoonbank.com

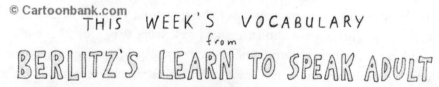

When we read, we usually read a special form of Standard English that differs from spoken, conversational language in many ways. Scholars call this academic language, book language, or literate language. It uses more stylistic formalities, is less repetitious, and is more carefully constructed. Phrases are not punctuated with "uh," "like," "you know," or repetitions of words. Vocabulary tends to be precise, unusual, descriptive, and topic-specific. Sentences may be long and complex, with embedded clauses or compounding of independent clauses. Sentences may be joined together with subordinating or coordinating conjunctions that indicate the logic of the ideas presented. Paragraphs—especially in expository text—have main ideas, details, and transition sentences. All meaning must be expressed in the words themselves because the person who reads cannot depend on the redundant cues (e.g., tone of voice, gestures, facial expressions) that are present during personal conversations.

That new forms of language must be mastered for reading and writing adds to the challenge. A reader encounters a different language from that of conversation—the language of books and of academic discussion. The literate person has also learned to decipher the writing system with which that language is represented.

Exercise 2.1	Comparing Spoken and Written Language

- Complete the comparison of spoken (conversational) and written (literate) language in the following chart. (Some of the boxes are started or completed for you.)

- More text excerpts are provided after the chart to help you describe literate language.

	Spoken (Conversational) Language	Written, Academic, or Literate Language
Speech Sounds (phonology)	• Sounds are blended together in spoken words (coarticulated).	• Sounds are represented by alphabet letters. • Letters are isolated units. • Letters must be matched with sounds and sequentially processed, left to right, in space as well as time.
Vocabulary (semantics)	Casual Common Incomplete > liberty usage	uncommon specific, precise longer correct usage

(continued)

Exercise 2.1   (continued)

	Spoken (Conversational) Language	Written, Academic, or Literate Language
Sentence Structure (syntax)	• Sentences tend to be incomplete, run-on, or otherwise ungrammatical in conversational speech.	compound complex careful construction
Paragraphs and Discourse Structure	no P may be rambling, circular, repetitive, disorganized	• Paragraphs have a logical structure, especially in expository text. • Linking words, repeated phrases, and pronoun referents are used deliberately to make text "hang together." • Different paragraph organizations serve specific goals of logic. • Meaning must be clearly and completely put into words.
Overall Context for Use, and Feedback Available During Communication (pragmatics)	• Conversational speech is supported with gestures, facial expressions, tone of voice, and the presence of shared context or events.	meaning in words no contextual redundancy need to imagine "voice" + "intent"

From *Animal Farm: A Fairy Story* (Chapter IX)

By George Orwell

New York: Harcourt Brace, 1996 (originally published 1945)

   ... Meanwhile life was hard. The winter was as cold as the last one had been, and food was even shorter. Once again all rations were reduced, except those of the pigs and the dogs. A too rigid equality in rations, Squealer explained, would have been contrary to the principles of Animalism. In any case he had no difficulty in proving to the other animals that they were not in reality short of food, whatever the appearances might be. For the time being, certainly, it had been found necessary to make a readjustment of rations (Squealer always spoke of it as a "readjustment," never as a "reduction"), but in comparison with the days of Jones, the improvement was enormous.

Exercise 2.1   (continued)

From *Abe Lincoln Grows Up* (Chapter XVI)
By Carl Sandburg
New York: Harcourt Children's Books, 1985 (originally published 1926)

... At the Pigeon Creek settlement, while the structure of his bones, the build and hang of his torso and limbs, took shape, other elements, invisible, yet permanent, traced their lines in the tissues of his head and heart.

From *Peter Pan and Wendy* (Chapter Three)
By J. M. Barrie
New York: Henry Holt and Co., 2003 (originally published 1924)

... There was another light in the room now, a thousand times brighter than the night-lights, and in the time we have taken to say this, it has been in all the drawers in the nursery, looking for Peter's shadow, rummaged the wardrobe and turned every pocket inside out. It was not really a light; it made this light by flashing about so quickly, but when it came to rest for a second you saw it was a fairy, no longer than your hand, but still growing. It was a girl called Tinker Bell, exquisitely gowned in a skeleton leaf, cut low and square, through which her figure could be seen to the best advantage. She was slightly inclined to *embonpoint*.

From *Calculus: Graphical, Numerical, Algebraic*
By Ross L. Finney, Franklin Demana, Bert K. Waits, and Daniel Kennedy
Upper Saddle River, NJ: Pearson Prentice Hall, 2002

... The development of integral calculus starts from calculation of areas by a technique that leads to a natural definition of area as a limit of finite sums. The limits used to define areas are special cases of a kind of limit called a definite integral. Presenting the properties of definite integrals, developing numerical methods of computing definite integrals, and applying the numerical methods with a graphing calculator are central goals of this chapter.

What Is Special About an Alphabet?

Writing systems evolved slowly over many thousands of years (Comrie, Matthews, & Polinsky, 1996; Sacks, 2003). Alphabetic writing, first generated less than 5,000 years ago, is a very recent achievement in human evolution. About nine-tenths of the world's 4,000 to 6,000 existing spoken languages have no indigenous, or native, written form, let alone an alphabet.

The first writing systems were pictograms that directly represented, or made pictures of, the intended meaning. More abstract symbolic systems evolved, but they continued to use symbols to represent units of *meaning* (logographs) rather than units of *sound*. Mayan glyphs and ancient Chinese radicals were examples of logographic writing systems that did not employ an alphabet. Most early writing systems represented whole words, meaningful parts of words (morphemes), or syllables, rather than individual speech sounds.

Pictograms that directly represent meaning (hieroglyphics):

Logographs that abstractly represent meaning, not sound (Chinese radicals):

Syllabic symbols that directly represent whole syllables (Cherokee):

| sa | se | si | so | su | sʌ |

Alphabetic symbols that represent consonants and vowels, or individual phonemes (Greek, Russian):

αβχδεφγηιφκλ

б в г д е ж з и к л м н

Remarkably, alphabets in use today descend from a "mother" alphabet (see *Figure 2.1*). Since the first group of letters was invented somewhere in or around Egypt, nearly every successive alphabetic system used recycled letters and adapted them to represent the new language. The Greeks took and modified the Phoenician alphabet; the Etruscans and Romans took and modified the Greek alphabet, and so on.

Figure 2.1. Flowchart of the Evolution of Alphabetic Writing

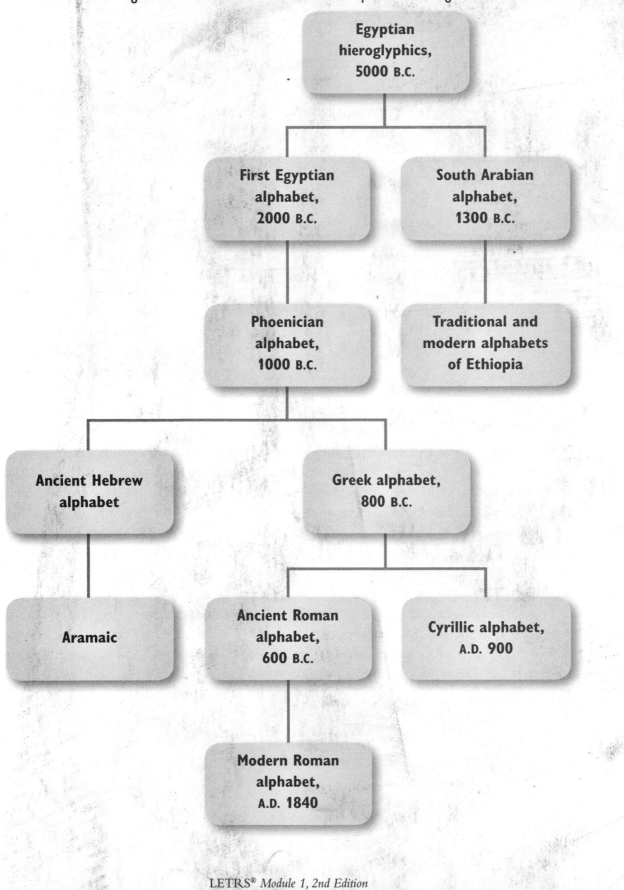

Awareness of Speech Sounds and the Alphabetic Principle

Figure 2.2. Types of Writing Systems

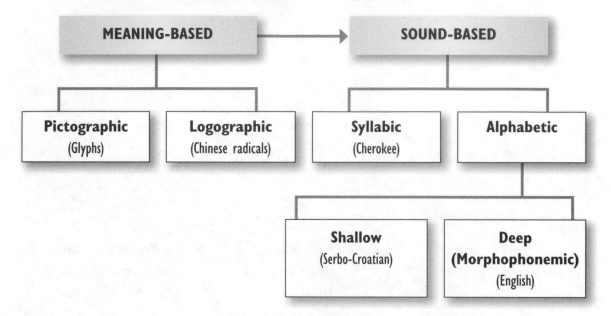

Shallow and Deep Orthographies

Writing systems (orthographies) can be classified according to the level of language they represent. *Figure 2.2* illustrates a continuum of representation, from meaning-based systems to sound-based systems. Sound-based systems can represent whole syllables or individual speech sounds. In addition, alphabetic systems can be "shallow" or "deep." (Note: These are *linguistic terms*, not value judgments.) In a "shallow" (or "transparent") alphabetic orthography (e.g., Finnish, Serbo-Croatian), the sound-symbol correspondences in the alphabetic writing system are regular and predictable, with one sound represented by one symbol or letter. Once we learn the sound that goes with a letter, we can read the words by using that code.

English, in contrast, is a "deep" (or "opaque") alphabetic orthography. Its spelling system represents morphemes (meaningful parts) as well as speech sounds. The term we use to describe how English is spelled by both speech sounds (phonemes) and meaningful units (morphemes) is **morphophonemic**. Consider these examples:

want<u>ed</u>, humm<u>ed</u>, pitch<u>ed</u>	<u>ri</u>te, <u>ri</u>tual
comp<u>ress</u>, comp<u>ress</u>ion	an<u>xi</u>ous, an<u>xi</u>ety
<u>na</u>tive, <u>na</u>tional, <u>na</u>tivity	

We tend to spell the meaningful parts of words (morphemes) the same way, regardless of their pronunciation. If English were a totally transparent orthography, **-ed** would be spelled the way it sounds. Instead, it has three pronunciations—/t/, /d/, and /əd/—that are all spelled the same way. The word **compression** uses stable spellings of the prefix *com-* and the root *press*, even though the prefix is unaccented, the vowel is indistinct (schwa), and the final **ss** in *press* sounds like /sh/. The spellings of **compress** and **compression** look the same and help us see these words as sharing meaningful parts.

Look at the other examples that are provided above. We spell these words by sound *and* by meaning. George Bernard Shaw once led a campaign to change English spelling to a more phonetic (or transparent) system, but his efforts failed because much would be lost if English spellings were changed. For example, it would become difficult to read English writings from centuries past if the spelling patterns were radically altered. In addition, stable spelling of meaningful word parts allows us to read and get to the meaning of words more quickly, which is the overall goal of reading. Nevertheless, it is impossible to read an alphabetic writing system unless one can mentally link the alphabetic symbols with the single speech sounds or phonemes that they represent. All alphabets require the reader to be aware of *speech sounds (phonemes)*.

Some teachers of Spanish believe that Spanish uses a syllabic writing system. In Spanish, spoken syllables often end with long vowel sounds, whereas in English, at least half of the syllables have short vowels and end in one or more consonants. Syllables in Spanish are often consonant-vowel sequences, such as **mi**, **me**, **ma**, **mo**, and **mu**, and are relatively easy to learn. In addition, many Spanish words are cognates that are built around the same Latin and Greek prefixes, suffixes, or roots that English words also employ. The common language ancestors of Spanish and English enable English speakers to readily recognize the meanings of Spanish words such as *problema, diagrama, universidad, aniversario, laborioso, abundante, técnico, turista, argumento, atención,* and *romántico.* Spanish writing is somewhat more transparent or decodable, with regard to its phonics system, than English. Even so, Spanish writing is not a syllabic system. Although syllable patterns are often taught, Spanish uses an alphabetic orthography that represents the sound or phonemic level of spoken language, and Spanish readers must also be aware of the individual speech sounds that letters represent.

The Cherokee language, on the other hand, is a true syllabary, with one symbol representing one whole syllable. Modern Japanese includes sound-based representations, both syllabic and alphabetic, added to Chinese characters, or radicals; it is a true amalgam of sound-based and meaning-based writing systems.

ENGLISH = MORPHOPHONEMIC

bound base   rupture

Advantages of an Alphabetic System

Why was the alphabet such a wonderful invention? Because any word could be read or written, using a small set of symbols. Armed with knowledge of the code, the learner could read without memorizing hundreds of unique signs or symbols. A limited number of symbols could be combined infinitely to represent an entire language. Language could be written down and read by anyone who could match the symbols to the sounds they represented.

"Now you're probably all asking yourselves, 'Why must I learn to read and write?' "

In spite of its utility, alphabetic writing eluded human invention until about 5,000 years ago and was not a common form of written communication until 3,000 years ago. The Phoenician alphabet, clearly established and used in the Middle East by 1100 B.C., was adapted by the Greeks and Romans; however, alphabetic writing was by no means universal until a few hundred years ago. Why? Because the existence of the phoneme—that which a letter represents—is not a self-evident, natural, or consciously accessible understanding for humans. People are "wired" instead to process speech for the meanings it conveys. Our brains are not adapted to read, but they are adapted to support learning to speak. The invention of the alphabet represented an astonishing achievement of metalinguistic awareness—that is, the ability to think about and reflect on the structure of language itself. Had insight into the building blocks of language been easily achieved, then alphabets would have been invented much more readily and used more widely.

Of all the alphabetic languages in the world, the writing system of English is comparatively difficult. Languages such as Spanish, Italian, Serbo-Croatian, and Finnish are more phonetic and more easily decoded than English. Those languages are closer to having one letter for each sound. "Congratulazioni per l'acuisto della stampante" can be read with relatively little difficulty if the vowel sounds are known to the reader, even if that person does not know the meanings of Italian words.

English sound-symbol correspondences are regular enough that we can read nonsense words as well as real words if we know alphabetic or phoneme-grapheme correspondences. Lewis Carroll's poem *Jabberwocky* in *Through The Looking Glass and What Alice Found There* (Carroll, 1993) can be read by anyone who knows the phonic code, even though it has little (or no?) meaning:

> *'Twas brillig, and the slithy toves*
> *Did gyre and gimble in the wabe;*
> *All mimsy were the borogoves,*
> *And the mome raths outgrabe.*

Do you remember how you learned to read? *Exercise 2.2* will briefly put you in the shoes of a novice reader.

Cut out these symbol cards so that you can manipulate them, or make your own by copying the symbols onto sticky notes. You will use these symbols in *Exercise 2.2*.

θ	ʌ	ŋ
I	š	ċ
k	f	t
w	n	

Cut out these sight word cards so that you can manipulate them, or make your own by copying the words onto sticky notes. You will use these words in *Exercise 2.2*.

ð<u>ə</u>	<u>w</u>ʌ<u>z</u>	<u>æ</u>nd
<u>ə</u>	<u>aj</u>	<u>tu</u>
<u>ju</u>	<u>ʌv</u>	

Exercise 2.2 Simulation of Learning to Read

- After completing this exercise, be prepared to share your reflections.
- Follow your instructor, who will be using the script in *Appendix A*, as you are guided through these activities:

  a. **Phoneme awareness**: Imitate the correct production of each phoneme. Describe how each one is articulated.

  b. **Phoneme-grapheme association**: Match phonemes with symbols. Match symbols with phonemes.

  c. **Blend** sounds into words.

  d. **Memorize** some of these sight words so that sentence reading is possible.

  e. **Read** words, phrases, and sentences.

  f. **Spell** words with letter tiles.

  g. **Write** symbols for sounds that are dictated.

  h. **Practice**. Make a word chain. Build fluency in word recognition.

  i. **Read** a story with sounds and words that have been taught.

1. Select or make the following letter tiles:

f	k	n	ŋ	θ	š	I

2. Select or make word cards for the following irregular sight words:

<u>**ænd**</u>	<u>ə</u>	<u>ðə</u>	<u>wʌz</u>

3. Review the sounds /f/, /k/, /n/, and symbols *f, k, n.*

4. Learn these four new sounds—/ŋ/, /θ/, /š/, /I/—and their symbols. Practice listening for the sounds, pointing to the symbols, and saying the sounds for the symbols.

5. Blend these sounds into words:

I n	θ I n	θ I ŋ	f I š
f I n	š I n	θ I k	
k I n	k I ŋ	k I k	

(continued)

Exercise 2.2   (continued)

6. Read these words with consonant blends:

kɪŋk	ɪŋk	fɪŋk	θɪŋk

7. Read these irregular whole sight words:

<u>ænd</u>	ə	<u>ðə</u>	<u>wʌz</u>

8. Read these phrases and sentences:

θɪk <u>ænd</u> θɪn

<u>wʌz</u> ə fɪŋk

θɪŋk ɪn ɪŋk

kɪk <u>ðə</u> šɪn

kɪŋk <u>ðə</u> θɪŋ

fɪšɪŋ <u>wʌz</u> ə kɪk.

<u>ðə</u> kɪŋ <u>wʌz</u> fɪšɪŋ.

<u>ðə</u> kɪŋ <u>wʌz</u> θɪn.

<u>ðə</u> fɪš fɪn <u>wʌz</u> θɪn.

<u>wʌz</u> <u>ðə</u> θɪŋ ə fɪš?

9. Spell with letter tiles. Write the words you spell on these lines:

_____

_____

_____

10. Write the dictated words, phrases, and sentences.

<u>θɪk šɪn   ðə fɪš fɪn wʌz</u>
<u>θɪk ænd θɪn   θɪk.</u>
<u>θɪŋk θɪn</u>
<u>ðə kɪŋ wʌz fɪšɪŋ</u>

Exercise 2.2   (continued)

11. Learn these additional sounds and symbols:

w	t	ċ

12. Listen. Write the symbol:

_____

_____

13. Read these regular words:

ċn	ċf	tċŋ	tċk
θċt	tċt	fċt	kċt
θċŋ	kċŋ	kċf	wċnt
wIš	wIŋ	wIn	wIθ
wIkIŋ		wċkIŋ	

14. Learn these additional irregular whole words:

<u>aj</u>	<u>tu</u>	<u>ju</u>

15. Read these phrases and sentences:

a. θIŋk, tċk, <u>ænd</u> wċk

b. wċnt <u>ænd</u> wIš

c. θIŋk <u>ðə</u> θċt

d. tċkIŋ ċn <u>ænd</u> ċf

e. <u>ðə</u> kIŋ kċt ə kċf.

f. kIŋ kċn fċt ċf <u>ðə</u> θIŋ.

g. <u>aj</u> wċnt <u>tu</u> fIš wIθ <u>ju</u>.

h. <u>ju</u> wċkt θIŋkIŋ θċts ċn <u>ænd</u> ċf.

(continued)

Exercise 2.2   (continued)

16. Learn this new sound-symbol correspondence and this new sight word:

Λ	ΛV (of)

17. Read this story:

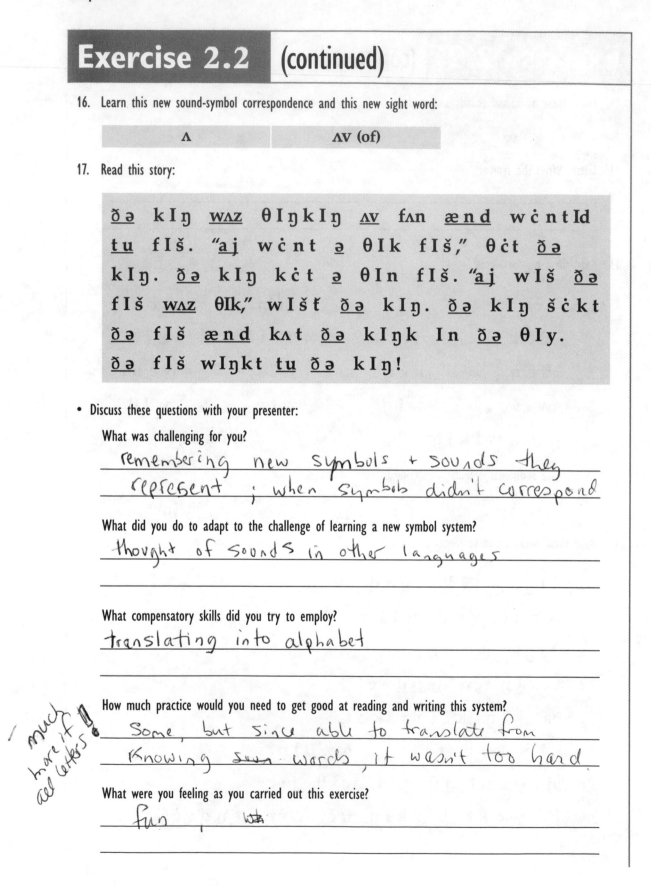

ðə kIŋ <u>wʌz</u> θIŋkIŋ <u>ʌv</u> fʌn ænd wċntId <u>tu</u> fIš. "<u>aj</u> wċnt ə θIk fIš," θċt <u>ðə</u> kIŋ. <u>ðə</u> kIŋ kċt ə θIn fIš. "<u>aj</u> wIš <u>ðə</u> fIš <u>wʌz</u> θIk," wIšť <u>ðə</u> kIŋ. <u>ðə</u> kIŋ šċkt <u>ðə</u> fIš <u>ænd</u> kʌt <u>ðə</u> kIŋk In <u>ðə</u> θIy. <u>ðə</u> fIš wIŋkt <u>tu</u> <u>ðə</u> kIŋ!

Λ

Ω

• Discuss these questions with your presenter:

What was challenging for you?

remembering new symbols + sounds they represent ; when symbols didn't correspond

What did you do to adapt to the challenge of learning a new symbol system?

thought of sounds in other languages

What compensatory skills did you try to employ?

translating into alphabet

How much practice would you need to get good at reading and writing this system?

much more if all letters

Some, but since able to translate from knowing some words, it wasn't too hard.

What were you feeling as you carried out this exercise?

fun, with

Take 2 Review

- Complete this two-column organizer.
- In the first column are restatements of main ideas. Work with the group or your partner to complete the second column. List a few details that elaborate the main ideas or that state the relevance of those ideas for your school or classroom.

Knowledge/Main Ideas	Application/Details
1. Compared to speaking, which is natural, learning to read is not natural.	
2. Academic, or "book," language differs from conversational, spoken language.	
3. English orthography is *morphophonemic*, which means that it is a "deep" alphabetic writing system organized by both letter-sound correspondences and morphology.	

Chapter 3

What the Brain Does When It Reads

Learner Objectives for Chapter 3

- Survey the skills that support proficient reading.
- Understand what eye movement studies reveal about reading.
- Identify and describe the role of four major brain-processing systems in recognizing printed words.
- Contrast the Four-Part Processing model with a cueing systems model.

Warm-Up: Watch Eye Movements

- Working with a partner, take turns watching each other's eyes during oral reading of a paragraph or two of this book.

Eye Movements and Reading

You have just watched the eyes of a person scanning text at a normal rate. The eye seems to be ahead of the voice when we read aloud—and indeed, it is. The precision eye-movement research of scientists such as Rayner and Pollatsek (1989) at the Massachusetts Institute of Technology showed in many experiments over 20 years that the reading eye fixates on most content words (especially nouns and verbs) in a rapid series of stops and jumps called *fixations* and *saccades*. When fixated, the eye rests for about .25 seconds (250 milliseconds) on a content word and takes in a span of about seven to nine letters to the right of the fixation and three to four letters to the left before it jumps over to the next fixation point. More letters are processed to the right of the fixation if the eye is scanning from left to right. The opposite would be true for reading a language that is scanned from right to left, such as Hebrew or Arabic.

Figure 3.1 What the Eye Takes in During Fixations

```
Eye_movement exxxxxxxxxxxxxxxxxxxxxxxxxxxxxxxxxxxxxxxxxxxxxxxxxxx
xxxxxxvement experimxxxxxxxxxxxxxxxxxxxxxxxxxxxxxxxxxxxxxxxxxxxxxx
xxxxxxxxxxxxexperimentationxxxxxxxxxxxxxxxxxxxxxxxxxxxxxxxxxxxxxxxx
xxxxxxxxxxxxxxxxxxmentation in axxxxxxxxxxxxxxxxxxxxxxxxxxxxxxxxxxxx
xxxxxxxxxxxxxxxxxxxxxxion_in a laborxxxxxxxxxxxxxxxxxxxxxxxxxxxxxxxx
xxxxxxxxxxxxxxxxxxxxxxxxxxxxx_a_laboratory xxxxxxxxxxxxxxxxxxxxxxxxx
xxxxxxxxxxxxxxxxxxxxxxxxxxxxxxxxxxxoratory settingxxxxxxxxxxxxxxxxxx
xxxxxxxxxxxxxxxxxxxxxxxxxxxxxxxxxxxxxxxxxx_setting aids xxxxxxxxxxx
xxxxxxxxxxxxxxxxxxxxxxxxxxxxxxxxxxxxxxxxxxxxxxxng_aids in our xxxx
```

- **Bold** letters represent **fixations**—what the eye is seeing directly in its *foveal* view.

- Underlined letters represent what is subconsciously processed during a fixation, not what we see directly. This is referred to as our *parafoveal* view and gives us partial information of what is to come next.

- The complete sentence: *Eye movement experimentation in a laboratory setting aids in our understanding of the reading process.*

Although we may not be aware of it, we do not skip over words, read print selectively, or recognize words by sampling a few letters of the print, as whole language theorists proposed in the 1970s. Reading is accomplished with letter-by-letter processing of the word (Rayner, Foorman, Perfetti, Pesetsky, & Seidenberg, 2001, 2002). Fluent readers *do* perceive each and every letter of print. Thus, we can distinguish **casual** from **causal**, **grill** from **girl**, and **primeval** from **prime evil**. Better readers process the internal details of printed words and match them to the individual speech sounds that make up the spoken word. Even when "chunks" are recognized, they can be analyzed into their individual phoneme-grapheme correspondences on demand.

Some children do have inherent vision problems, but they are independent of the types of problems that can be causes of reading difficulty. Visual acuity problems, such as near-sightedness, certainly should be identified and treated with corrective lenses, but language-based reading problems will not be cured with vision therapies. For example, there is no evidence that colored lenses or overlays relieve language-based reading problems or that eye-movement therapy is effective as a substitute for reading instruction. Faulty eye movements or visual fatigue most often are symptoms, not causes, of reading difficulty.

Eye movement studies have shown that mature, proficient readers do not skip words, use context to process words, or bypass phonics in establishing word recognition. Reading requires letter-wise processing of print and the ability to match symbols with the speech sounds they represent.

Proficient Reading Depends on Many Skills

The mechanics of fluent, accurate reading are quite remarkable. A proficient reader appears to scan the print effortlessly, extracting meaning and sifting through it, making connections between new ideas in the text and existing knowledge, and interpreting according to his or her purposes. The proficient reader figures out new words and names very quickly and with minimal effort, consciously sounding out new words if necessary. New words are decoded with minimal effort because the sounds, syllables, and meaningful parts of words are recognized automatically. If the good reader happens to misread a word or phrase or does not comprehend a word or phrase, he or she quickly adapts by rereading to make sense of the information and clarify what was unclear. As she reads along, the reader forms a mental model, or schema, for the meanings just extracted, linking new information to background knowledge. That schema, or mental construction, has a logical framework into which she files the information to remember. Reading is a complex mental activity!

The attainment of reading skill has fascinated psychologists and invited more study than any other aspect of human cognition because of its social importance and its complexity. The study of proficient reading and reading problems earned more funding increases from Congress in the 1990s than any other public health issue studied by the National Institute of Child Health and Human Development (Lyon & Chhabra, 2004). As a consequence of programmatic research efforts over many years, scientific consensus on some important issues in reading development and reading instruction has been reached (McCardle & Chhabra, 2004; Rayner et al., 2001).

SVR

multiplied
X = not
additive

Figure 3.2 Two Domains and Five Essential Components of Reading

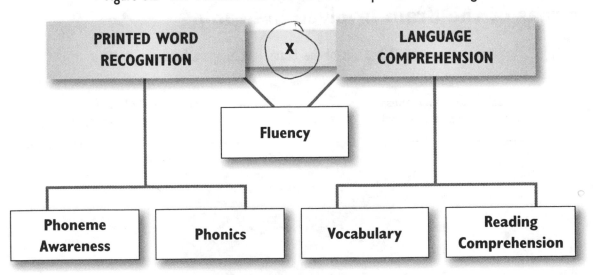

One important result of research is the finding that fluent reading for comprehension depends on the ability to recognize and attach meaning to individual words. Reading is the product of two major sets of subskills: *printed word recognition* and *language comprehension*. Printed words cannot be interpreted unless they are accurately pronounced or named (e.g., **abroad** is not **aboard**; **scarred** is not **scared**; **etymology** is not **entomology**). Pronouncing or decoding a word requires knowledge of the sounds in words (*phoneme awareness*) and the alphabetic system by which we represent those sounds (*phonics*). The meanings of those sounds must be recognized at the word level (*vocabulary*) and at the level of connected language (*text comprehension*).

A *fluent* reader carries out the process of word–naming with deceptive ease. A fluent reader recognizes or names words so rapidly and effortlessly that he or she is not aware of those mental processes. Automatic word recognition frees up cognitive resources (i.e., attention, self-monitoring, working memory) that can then be applied to comprehension. A short list of some major subskills of reading, then, is as follows:

- Phoneme awareness
- Use of phonics to decode words accurately
- Automatic recognition of words previously deciphered
- Knowledge of what most words mean
- Understanding sentences and language of books
- Constructing meaning (connecting ideas in the text and with each other and with prior knowledge)
- Monitoring comprehension and rereading or rethinking if miscomprehension occurs.

Four Processing Systems That Support Word Recognition

Areas of the Brain Involved in Reading

Figure 3.3 Areas of the Brain That Support Reading

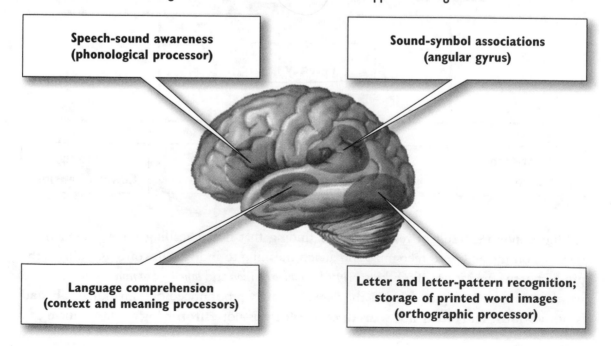

Speech-sound awareness
(phonological processor)

Sound-symbol associations
(angular gyrus)

Language comprehension
(context and meaning processors)

Letter and letter-pattern recognition;
storage of printed word images
(orthographic processor)

In order for reading to occur, several major regions of the left half of the brain must perform specific jobs in concert with the others. In most people, language functions are subsumed by the left cerebral hemisphere, and the processing of written language depends on networks that are located primarily in the language centers. The networks that are highlighted in *Figure 3.3* include the **phonological processor** (in the back part of the *frontal lobe* of the brain); the **orthographic processor** (in the *lower back [occipital]* part of the brain); and the middle area (*temporal-parietal-occipital junction*, or **angular gyrus**), where these two processing systems communicate to support word recognition. In addition, pathways link the back and middle areas to the *temporal* areas, where **word meanings** and **connected language** are processed. Notice that the orthographic processor is on the side of the brain that serves language (left side) and that it is wired into the language centers. Learning to recognize words depends heavily on accurate matching of written symbols with sounds and the connection of those sound patterns with meaning.

Jobs of the Four Processing Systems

Figure 3.4 The Four-Part Processing Model for Word Recognition

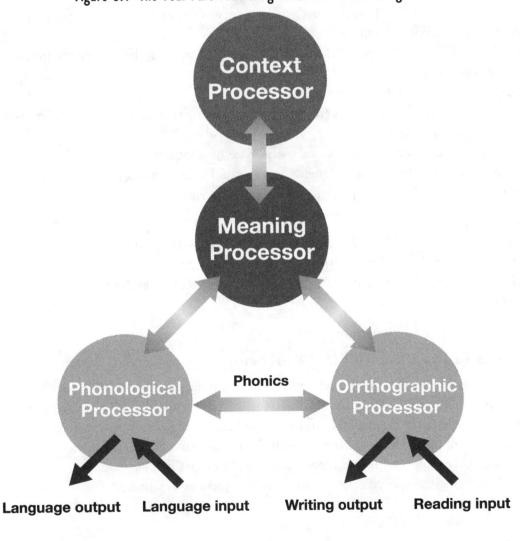

LETRS® Module 1, 2nd Edition

The schematic representation of the four brain-processing systems involved in word recognition (*Figure 3.4*) is based on cognitive psychological experimentation. It was originally proposed by Seidenberg and McClelland (1989) as a summation and synthesis of many experiments on the nature of skilled and unskilled reading. This model was developed before functional brain studies showed where and when these mental activities take place during reading (Berninger & Richards, 2002; Eden & Moats, 2002; Shaywitz, 2003). The model is discussed at length in Adams' (1990) landmark book, *Beginning to Read: Thinking and Learning About Print*, and two recent summary articles in *Psychological Science in the Public Interest* and *Scientific American* (Rayner, et al., 2001, 2002). The schematic representation of the systems simplifies the nature of skilled reading because several subcomponents within each processing system have also been identified (Vellutino et al., 2007).

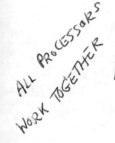

The four-part processor concept, although a simplification, is useful because it suggests: (a) the various ways in which reading problems might develop; and (b) why reading instruction should target several kinds of skills. The model reminds us that *instruction should aim to educate all of the processing systems and enable them to work together.* It shows why recognition and fast processing of sounds, letter patterns, and morphemes—as well as word meanings, language comprehension, and background knowledge—are all important components of skilled reading. The model also helps researchers decide what questions or hypotheses to test in scientific studies. For example:

- Is one processing system more important to educate than the others at a given stage of reading development?
- How do these systems interact?
- What kinds of experiences are necessary for each processing system to learn its job in the reading brain?
- Is it possible to be a good reader if one system is not functioning well?

Next, we will explore in more detail what each of the four processors is responsible for and how each one contributes to proficient reading and writing.

Exercise 3.1 Acting Out the Brain

- Follow your instructor as he or she walks you through the next section on the jobs of the four processing systems.

The Job of the Phonological Processor

This processing system enables us to perceive, remember, interpret, and produce the speech-sound system of our own language and learn the sounds of other languages. The phonological processor enables us to imitate and produce *prosody*, or the stress patterns, in speech, including the rise and fall of the voice during phrasing. It is responsible for such functions as:

- Mentally categorizing and identifying the phonemes in a language system;
- Producing the speech sounds and syllable sequences in words;

- Comparing and distinguishing words that sound similar (e.g., **reintegrate** vs. **reiterate**);
- Remembering and repeating the words in a phrase or the sounds in a word;
- Retrieving specific words from the mental dictionary (lexicon) and pronouncing them;
- Holding the sounds of a word in memory so that a word can be written down; and
- Taking apart the sounds in a word so that they can be matched with alphabetic symbols.

The phonological processor has many jobs, all of them related to the perception, memory, and production of speech. _Phoneme awareness_ is one job of the phonological processor. Children who have trouble with phonological processing show a variety of symptoms, such as difficulty remembering sounds for letters or blending them together, difficulty recognizing the subtle differences between similar words, and trouble spelling all the speech sounds in a word.

LETRS Module 2 is all about this processing system. The phonological processor is so important that it needs its own module!

The Job of the Orthographic Processor

The orthographic processing system receives visual input from printed words. It perceives and recognizes letters, punctuation marks, spaces, and the letter patterns in words. The orthographic processor enables us to copy lines of print, recognize words as whole units, or remember letter sequences for spelling. When we look at print, its features are filtered, identified, and matched to images of letters or letter sequences already in our orthographic memory. If the letters or letter sequences are familiar, we associate them with sounds and meanings.

Most people have no trouble interpreting widely varying print forms, including individual handwriting styles, type fonts, or uppercase and lowercase letters. The size, style, and case of print are not major factors in word recognition once a reader knows letters and letter-sound relationships. Letters are recognized by their distinguishing features, including curves, straight lines and angles.

The orthographic processing system stores information about print that is necessary for word recognition and spelling. The speed with which letters are recognized and recalled is very important for proficient reading. Obviously, print images must be associated with meaning for reading comprehension to occur. Children with orthographic processing weaknesses will have trouble forming "sight word" habits, will be poor spellers, and will often read slowly because they are sounding everything out long after they should be doing that.

LETRS Module 3 is all about the organization of English orthography (the information that the orthographic processor must learn), and Module 7 is devoted to the teaching of phonics. Additionally, Module 10 addresses the advanced skills of phonics and word study necessary for reading and spelling multisyllabic words in our language.

? >

The Job of the Meaning Processor

According to the four-part processing model, recognizing words as meaningful entities requires communication among the phonological processor, orthographic processor, and meaning processor. The meaning processor is also called the *semantic processor* because it interprets the meanings of words in and out of context. If we associate speech sounds with print symbols but do not access the meaning processor, we may read a foreign language (or our own!) without knowing what it means, read nonsense words, or read a new name by sounding it out but with no possibility of comprehension. The meaning processor stores the inventory of known words, organizes the mental dictionary or lexicon, and constructs the meanings of any new words that are named during reading. The context of the passage supports the construction of those meanings.

A word filed in your mental dictionary is a linguistic entity with many facets. When words are known in depth, their sounds, spellings, meaningful parts, typical uses, alternative meanings, and customary uses are known. The meaning processor is structured according to a number of semantic organization features such as synonym relationships, roots and other morphemes, spelling patterns, common meaning associations, and connotations. It expands and reorganizes itself as new vocabulary is learned.

In the lexicon, or mental dictionary, words are "filed" in meaning networks. Words are typically learned in relation to one another, not in isolation. We learn words best if we can connect them to something we already know. We learn words more readily if they are connected to images of their sounds and their spellings, as well as the contexts in which they are usually used. Children with weak vocabularies, limited knowledge of English, and/or weaknesses in verbal reasoning ability may have trouble reading. In these cases, children's decoding skills may or may not be better than their skills in meaning-making.

LETRS Module 4 is devoted to an exploration of word meanings and how to teach them.

The Job of the Context Processor

Refer back to page 33 and notice where the context processor is positioned in *Figure 3.4*. Its primary job is to interact with and provide support for the meaning processor. The term "context" refers to the sentence and sentence sequence in which a word is embedded, and the concepts or events that are being discussed or reported in the text. Context provides the referent for a word's meaning. Many same-sounding words have multiple meanings, but only one is correct when used within a specific sentence. For example, the spelling of a word such as **passed** or **past** is determined by its meaning in the context of a sentence:

- The quarterback **passed** the ball to the receiver for the touchdown.
- Champions of the **past** were guests at the start of the game.

Context may help us find or figure out a word's intended meaning if we do not already know the word. Context also enriches our knowledge of how each word is typically used in our language system. Context will resolve ambiguities associated with multiple meanings of many words. Context may also help us catch decoding errors and cause us to reread for

clarification. Well-developed background knowledge and verbal abilities as well as adequate)
reading fluency enable readers to use context productively.

A major point about the function of context in word recognition is that it plays only a limited role in facilitating word-naming itself. Word recognition and pronunciation are primarily the job of the phonological and orthographic processors. Students cannot comprehend text if they cannot read it accurately and fluently!

Module 6 of LETRS covers the topic of comprehension for young students; LETRS Module 11 addresses research and instructional practices best used for grades 4 and beyond.

Exercise 3.2 | The Four Processors at Work in the Classroom

- Walk through this exercise with your instructor. First, fill in the correct labels for the processors in the diagram on the next page: *phonological, orthographic, meaning,* and *context.*

- After labeling each processing system in the diagram, match each numbered task below to the processor(s) that is most obviously activated while the task is performed. Place the task number alongside the processor(s). Your presenter will do the first one with you.

  1. Decode and pronounce the unfamiliar printed word **chimera**.

  2. Repeat the *spoken* phrase "Riki-tiki tembo no serembo."

  3. Orally give a synonym for the word **anthology**.

  4. Read a passage to determine which meaning of the word **affirmative** is intended.

  5. Determine whether the spoken words **does** and **rose** end with the same speech sound.

  6. Underline all the words on a page in which the letter **c** is followed by **e, i,** or **y**.

  7. Write this sentence: *My mental lexicon craves enrichment.*

  8. Read and comprehend the next paragraph of this book.

(continued)

Exercise 3.2 (continued)

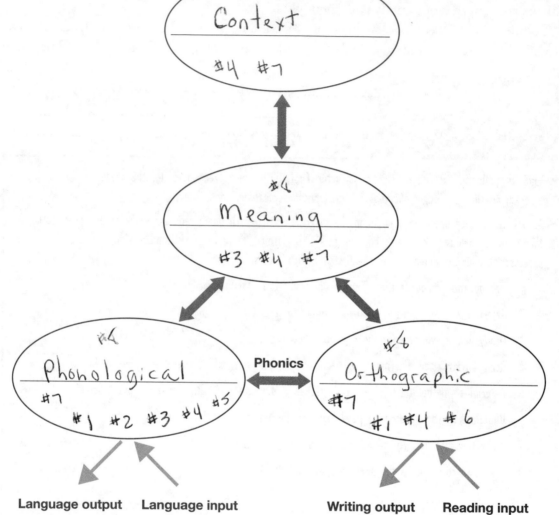

Context #6
#4 #7

Meaning #6
#3 #4 #7

Phonological #6
#7 #1 #2 #3 #4 #5

Phonics

Orthographic #6
#7 #1 #4 #6

Language output   Language input   Writing output   Reading input

Exercise 3.2 (Alternative)   Processing Systems and Classroom Instruction

- On a blank piece of paper, write out an activity you typically do with your class as you teach reading.
- Crumple the paper and throw your "snowball" into the center of the room. Your presenter will let you know what to do next.
- Are all processing systems addressed? Is one aspect of reading given more emphasis than another?

Moving Beyond Cueing Systems

In the early 1980s, an alternative conception about the nature of reading was promoted in the non-scientific literature on reading instruction, although the origin of this model is unclear (Adams, 1998). Known as the "Three Cueing Systems" model, it proposed that word recognition depended on three systems of linguistic cues that reside in a text. The model proposed that these three systems are used during reading as needed to decode words: (1) a *graphophonic* (visual) system; (2) a *semantic* (meaning) system; and (3) a *syntactic* system that provides linguistic context to process words in sentences. The cueing systems model was embedded in the miscue analysis procedure in "running records" or oral reading assessments and also was used as a rationale for whole-language approaches to reading instruction.

The Seidenberg and McClelland (1989) Four-Part Processing model departs from the Three Cueing Systems model in several critical ways. In the Four-Part Processing model, which converges with modern brain science, the phonological processor is separate and distinct from the orthographic processor. Each is only indirectly influenced by or driven by context. To educate the phonological processor and the orthographic processor, we teach children about speech sounds and print patterns, and then teach them how the two are linked. Accurately read words are then associated with meaning and placed in context.

In the Three Cueing Systems model, the phonological and orthographic processing systems are unified and characterized as "visual" instead of linguistic. The role of phonological processing in word recognition is minimized and obscured because it does not exist in the diagram. Teachers are not helped to understand or teach phonology directly, and teachers are encouraged to use meaning and context *as a replacement for* systematic instruction in the alphabetic code.

The Three Cueing Systems model overemphasizes the usefulness of context and meaning in word recognition. It encourages teachers to say to students who are stuck on a word, "What would make sense here?" before they expect the student to decode the word or blend the sounds together. It encourages teachers to believe that phonics strategies are a last resort and that systematic phonics instruction is unnecessary because children can rely on meaning to figure out words. The cueing model fosters dependence on pictures, prereading rehearsal, and context for identifying words. Unfortunately, these are the strategies that poor readers rely on when they are having difficulty deciphering the alphabetic code.

The Four-Part Processing model explains why a systematic, organized approach to teaching sounds and spellings is necessary and productive for many children. Until decoding skills are known, the most productive prompt to a student who is stumbling on a word is, "Look carefully at all the letters. Sound it out. Does that make sense?" Guessing at words on the basis of context, even with reference to an initial consonant sound, is not a good habit to encourage when children are first learning to read. Later reading fluency

---

Teaching Tips

What to say when a student stumbles on a word:
- "Look carefully at all letters."
- "Sound it out."
- "Does that word make sense?"

Avoid asking "What word makes sense here?" as your initial cue!

depends on early mastery of associations between letters, letter patterns, and speech sounds. Moreover, context use is an accurate way to identify unknown words only about one out of four to one out of ten times!

Take 2 Review

- Complete this two-column organizer.
- In the first column are restatements of main ideas. Work with the group or your partner to complete the second column. List a few details that elaborate the main ideas or that state the relevance of those ideas for your school or classroom.

Knowledge/Main Ideas	Application/Details
1. Good readers process *all* the letters in printed words; they read words completely and accurately.	
2. Four processing systems must work together to support printed word recognition.	

How Children Learn to Read and Spell

Learner Objectives for Chapter 4

- Describe how decoding and comprehension contribute to reading skill over time.
- Become familiar with the conceptions of reading development by Scarborough (2001), Chall (1996), and Ehri and Snowling (2004).
- Examine children's writing, spelling, and reading, and describe the phases of development for each skill.

Warm-Up: Look Closely at Spelling

- Here are two writing samples[2] from the same kindergarten student; the first sample was obtained in September, and the second sample was obtained in April of the following year.
- What has happened? What can the student do after eight months of excellent instruction that he could not do at the beginning of kindergarten?

Student C: Writing sample, September

a wich toock the pretty pretty princess and shee brot the princess and thennti wich toock the priness in to the cich in and the wich tide the princess to a char and then a prince savd her and then thae livd haplee evr aftr

Student C: Writing sample, the following April

---

[2] Kindergarten writing samples provided by Pat Tyborowski (Tyborowski & Crosby, 2001).

The Continuum of Reading and Spelling Development

The Developing Reading Brain

Models of proficient reading and an understanding of the many cognitive systems that support it do not tell us how people learn to read. Researchers have, however, investigated how the nature of skilled reading changes over time. At the end point, the proficient reader has learned to recognize words and interpret text rapidly, accurately, and often effortlessly. All processors are functioning and support reading. However, the role that each processor plays in reading development and the functional relationships among the processing systems change as reading skill develops.

Figure 4.1 Reading Levels and Reliance on Different Regions of the Brain

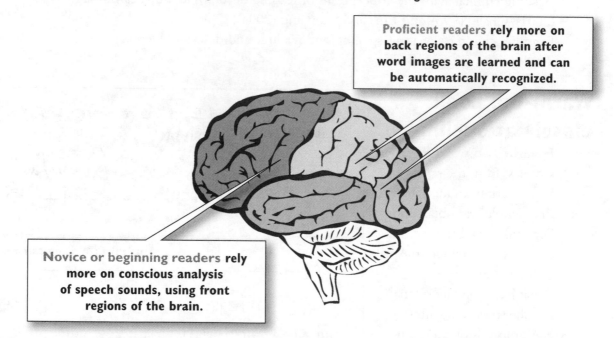

Proficient readers **rely more on back regions of the brain after word images are learned and can be automatically recognized.**

Novice or beginning readers **rely more on conscious analysis of speech sounds, using front regions of the brain.**

Good readers' brain activation patterns change with experience in reading. When children first learn to read, they are novices who must learn each component skill. During this time (refer to *Figure 4.1*), novice readers show greater activation in frontal and parieto-temporal (front to mid-back, left side) regions than skilled readers do because they must dismantle words for step-by-step, sound-symbol analysis. Novice good readers are aware of the sound-symbol connections in words and can use those to sound out words.

With practice and reading experience, however, good readers' brain patterns change slightly. More experienced good readers become more reliant on the occipito-temporal (farther back, left side) region to recognize words. They are more fluent because word recognition is automatic. At this stage of experienced good reading, readers often think that they are reading "by sight." While experienced good readers still activate the sounds in words and use phonics to decode words, they are unaware of this happening. Word recognition becomes a subconscious process, freeing up attention so that the reader can focus on the ultimate goal of reading, which is to understand what is being read.

The Connecticut Longitudinal Study

The two major subcomponents of reading—word recognition and text comprehension—change in relationship to each other between grades 1 and 8 (Foorman et al., 1997; Tannenbaum, Torgesen, & Wagner, 2006; Torgesen, 2005). Started in 1983 at the Yale University School of Medicine, the Connecticut Longitudinal Study (Foorman et al., 1997; Shankweiler, et al., 1999; Shaywitz, 2003) randomly selected a sample of 445 kindergarten children in various Connecticut public schools and tracked their progress for more than 20 years. Each child was tested yearly with the Woodcock-Johnson Achievement Test reading subtests (Woodcock & Johnson, 1989), which includes tests of word reading (real and nonsense words) and a test of passage comprehension. *Table 4.1* shows how the relative importance of word reading skill to passage reading comprehension changed over time.

Table 4.1 How the Relationship Between Decoding and Comprehension Changes Over Time
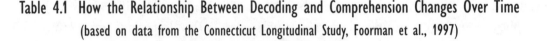
(based on data from the Connecticut Longitudinal Study, Foorman et al., 1997)

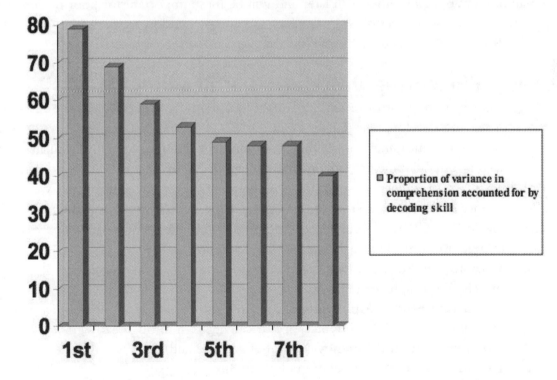

☐ Proportion of variance in comprehension accounted for by decoding skill

The correlations between these two components of reading changed as students learned to read. The correlations reflect the strength of association between decoding and comprehension. Initially, the ability to decode—the ability to read the words accurately—accounted for about 80 percent of passage reading comprehension ability. (The proportion of variance accounted for in one variable by another variable is obtained by squaring a correlation between the two.) Phonic decoding and fast word recognition were the most important tasks for first-grade students to master if they were going to be able to read a simple text passage and understand it. Passage comprehension at that level depended almost entirely on the ability to read single words accurately.[3]

By fourth grade, about 50 percent of the ability to comprehend passages was accounted for by the ability to read the words and apply phonics in word reading. As students progressed, comprehension of text depended more and more on other skills such as verbal reasoning, background knowledge, and knowledge of academic language. The Connecticut Longitudinal Study did not assess reading fluency. Torgesen (2005), at the Florida Center for Reading Research, has shown that verbal reasoning, topic knowledge, and language ability become even more important than fluency as students progress beyond the fifth grade.

These findings and others (Connor, Morrison, & Underwood, 2007) make it clear that the teaching of reading is not simply an equal "balance" of all subskills at each grade level. Rather, expert teachers know what subskills and processing capabilities to emphasize for which grade levels in order to get to the end goal of reading, which is comprehension. Many instructional approaches acknowledge the importance of all reading subskills, but an equal balance is not necessarily what gets the best results. Rather, the subskills of word recognition (i.e., phonology, letter naming, phonics, and word attack) should receive more emphasis early in reading development rather than later and will be more important for poor readers than good readers as students get older. Vocabulary and comprehension are important targets for reading instruction no matter what the student's age.

Chall's Pioneering Description of Reading "Stages"

Jeanne Chall, a professor of reading at Harvard for many years, developed the first-stage theory of reading development (Chall, 1996). Dr. Chall argued that "reading" was a word with very different meanings for children and adults of different ages and skill levels. In brief, her conceptual outline of reading stages differentiated the characteristics and demands of reading in six major periods of reading development. Her stages described well what children typically had to master as they progressed through a school curriculum. Chall's stage framework is still useful in understanding how the challenges of learning and teaching reading change over time. Her stages were defined as follows:

0 **Prereading**; also called *Prealphabetic*, *Logographic*, and *Preconventional* (typical of preschool through late kindergarten)

1 **Initial Reading** or **Alphabetic Decoding**; also called *Alphabetic Decoding Stage for Learning to Read Words* (typical of late kindergarten through early grade 2)

2 **Confirmation and Fluency** (typical of grades 2 and 3)

3 **Reading to Learn** (typical of grades 4 to 8)

4 **Multiple Points of View** (typical of high school)

5 **Construction and Reconstruction** (typical of college and adulthood)

---

[3] An analogy to math learning and teaching may be helpful here. To teach division, we first teach underlying skills, including number sense, addition, subtraction, multiplication, and place value. Reading comprehension depends on children recognizing words accurately.

Subsequent reading research has modified Chall's framework, especially in the areas of early word recognition and spelling. Current theories of early word-reading development emphasize the simultaneous and reciprocal growth of skill in all major processing systems (Ehri, 1996; Ehri & Snowling, 2004; Rayner et al., 2001; Stanovich, 2001) and the "amalgamation" of sound, spelling, and meaning in word learning. Phonological processing, orthographic processing, and meaning-making develop on a continuum, in tandem. Fluency is an essential component of skill development at each stage of learning. Verbal comprehension and vocabulary develop from the time children are infants. Exposure to text and reading practice are critical in moving the growth process along.

Ehri's Model of Reading Progression

Ehri's phases of word-reading development (Ehri, 1996; Ehri & Snowling, 2004), summarized in *Figure 4.2*, are widely referenced because their description rests on multiple experiments conducted over many years that have been replicated by other researchers. In Ehri's model, the ability to recognize many words "by sight" during fluent reading rests on the ability to map phonemes to graphemes or to master the alphabetic principle.

At first, children may recognize a few words as wholes by their configuration or the context in which they are found, such as on labels, boxes, or lists. However, progress in reading an alphabetic system occurs only if children learn how letters and sounds are connected. It is impossible for children to memorize more than a few dozen words without insight into the purpose of alphabetic symbols. Alphabetic learning is acquired through progressive differentiation of both the sounds in words and the letter sequences in print. Phoneme awareness is the foundation upon which letter-sound association can be constructed.

Figure 4.2 Ehri's Phases of Word-Reading Development

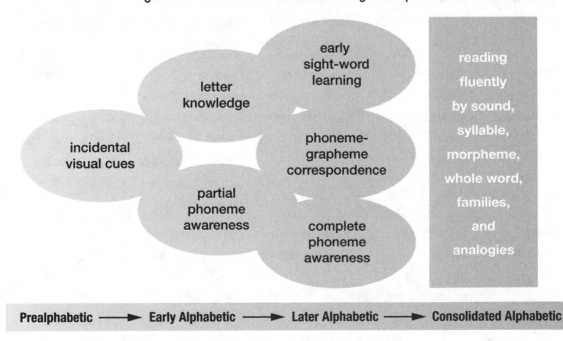

Prealphabetic ⟶ Early Alphabetic ⟶ Later Alphabetic ⟶ Consolidated Alphabetic

As students learn phoneme-grapheme mapping, their orthographic processors begin to store memories for recurring letter patterns in the form of "chunks"—syllable spellings, common endings and word parts, and high-frequency words. Accurate and fluent perception of chunks, however, rests on phoneme-grapheme mapping.

Table 4.2 documents the phases of gradual integration of information from the four processing systems that underlie word recognition. To illustrate, children at the beginning decoding stage, who have been exposed often to print in books, often show surprising awareness of the letter sequences and orthographic patterns that characterize English spelling. They may not associate familiar letters and letter sequences with speech sounds, but they know something about the sequences of letters in print just from looking at so many examples (Treiman & Bourassa, 2000). For example, they may know that –**ck** is used at the ends, not at the beginnings, of words; that letters can be doubled at the ends, not at the beginnings, of words; that only certain letters are doubled; and that syllables typically contain a vowel letter. Orthographic knowledge, or knowledge of the spelling system itself, develops when children have internalized an awareness of the sounds in words to which the letters correspond.

Table 4.2 Phases of Reading and Spelling Development
(based on Ehri & Snowling, 2004)

	Prealphabetic phase	Early Alphabetic phase	Later Alphabetic phase	Consolidated Alphabetic phase
How a child reads familiar words	Rote learning of incidental visual features of a word; no letter-sound awareness	Partial use of letter-sound correspondence; initial sound and salient consonants	Pronunciation of whole words on the basis of complete phoneme-grapheme mapping	Reads variously by phonemes, syllabic units, morpheme units, and whole words
How a child reads unfamiliar words	Guessing is constrained by context or memory of text	Constrained by context; gets first sound and guesses	Full use of phoneme-grapheme correspondence; blends all sounds left to right; begins to use analogy to known patterns	Sequential and hierarchical decoding; notices familiar parts first, reads by analogy to similar known words
Other indicators	Dependent on context; few words; errors and confusions; cannot read text	Similar-appearing words are confused	Rapid, unitized reading of whole familiar words is increasing	Remembers multisyllabic words; analogizes easily, associates word structure with meaning

(continued)

	Prealphabetic phase	Early Alphabetic phase	Later Alphabetic phase	Consolidated Alphabetic phase
Spelling	Strings letters together, assigns meaning without representing sounds in words	Represents a few salient sounds, such as beginning and ending consonants; fills in other letters randomly; knows some letter names for sounds	Phonetically accurate; beginning to incorporate conventional letter sequences and patterns; sight-word knowledge is increasing	Word knowledge includes language of origin; morphemes; syntactic role; ending rules; prefix, suffix, and root forms

Case Study Examples of Early Reading and Spelling Development

Prealphabetic Reading and Spelling

Figure 4.3 Prealphabetic Writing

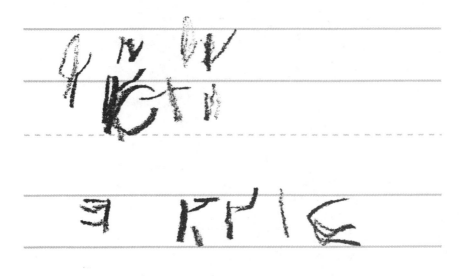

Many children come to kindergarten as prealphabetic readers and spellers, especially children from homes that do not provide them with exposure to books, reading aloud, or early instruction in the alphabet. In contrast, children with rich preschool experiences may move beyond this stage very early, by age 3 or 4. Sometimes this stage is called "logographic"

or "incidental visual cue" reading and writing because children memorize words by their appearance.

The kindergartener whose writing is displayed in *Figure 4.3* may not yet understand the alphabetic principle—the concept that letters represent speech sounds. The letters are not fully recognizable and look like marks designed simply to fill up some space on the page. This child may have memorized the letters in his name (e.g., Kyle). On a DIBELS® (Good & Kaminski, 2005) assessment or an early screening test, this child may not know what he is being asked if the teacher poses, "What is the first *sound* in the word **dog**?" The child might answer, "Bow-wow!"

This child may not yet understand that individual speech sounds are the building blocks of spoken words. Nevertheless, he may begin to observe the visual characteristics of print, such as left to right progression, the spacing of words, the alternating patterns of letters, the use of capitals at the beginnings of words, or the fact that certain combinations exist. We do not know how many letter names this child may have learned; he may know some even though he does not understand how the letters represent the sounds. Children at this stage need to learn phoneme awareness and the concept that letters represent sounds.

Early Alphabetic Reading and Spelling

Figure 4.4 Early Alphabetic Writing

#	Child's writing	Target word
1.	red	red
2.	mks	name
3.	beD	bed
4.	had	lady
5.	fer	fish
6.	Net	men
7.	Bittl	boat
8.	gaitl	girl
9.	kerlD	color
10.	Arihkl	angry
11.	tku	thank you
12.	Pcragl	people
13.	GoD	dog
14.	BaKlg	boy

On DIBELS (Good & Kaminski, 2005) testing or early screening measures, this child (*Figure 4.4*) is likely to do well at identifying the initial sound in words but may be weak at blending all the sounds in an unknown word. This child will try to read by identifying the first sound and guessing from context. She is just learning how to segment or separate all of the sounds in simple spoken words and may confuse printed words that share letters. For example, the words **house**, **horse**, and **how** begin with the same two letters; unless the child can process *all* of the letters and sounds, she may mistake one word for another.

The early alphabetic-phase learner is ready to learn how each sound is typically spelled and how to blend letter-sound correspondences into simple words. For a few weeks, months, or even longer, a novice alphabetic reader might expend a good deal of attention and mental effort to break words apart, blend the sounds, and approach new words sound-by-sound as symbols are linked. As individual phoneme-grapheme associations are learned and used, they become rapid and automatic, and the new reader "chunks" them into patterns. After sufficient exposure and practice, whole words are recognized as units. This kind of "sight" word recognition, however, depends on the reader being able to rapidly process the internal details of the word, letter by letter and sound by sound, so as to store a complete image of the word in memory.

Exercise 4.1   Sounds in Letter Names

• Write out the sounds in each letter name. (Two are completed as examples for you to follow.)

A ____/ā/____   J ____/j/ /ā/____   S _____

B _____   K _____   T _____

C _____   L _____   U _____

D _____   M _____   V _____

E _____   N _____   W _____

F _____   O _____   X _____

G _____   P _____   Y _____

H _____   Q _____   Z _____

I _____   R _____

(continued)

Exercise 4.1 (continued)

Children in the early and later alphabetic stages of reading and spelling rely on letter names to derive sounds.

1. Which letter names do *not* have the sounds that the letters represent?

   _____

2. Which letter names and sounds are likely to be most easily confused?

   _____

3. Can you think of a sound that is *not* in any letter name?

   _____

Later Alphabetic Reading and Spelling

Figure 4.5 Later Alphabetic Writing

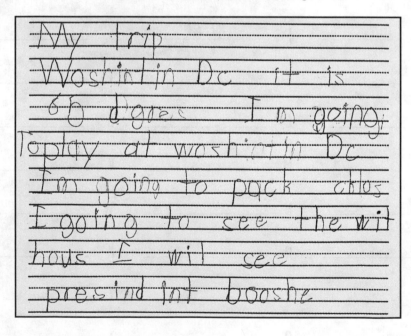

Children at the later alphabetic stage (*Figure 4.5*) will write fairly complete and reasonable phonetic spellings, showing that they can identify all of the sounds in words and know at least a common way to spell them. They sound out written words from left to right, applying what they have learned about phonics. As a consequence of accurate word identification, they store information about letter sequences in common words and syllable patterns. Thus, a "sight" vocabulary for reading begins to develop.

The instructional or learning goal of this stage is to build fast and accurate word recognition and spelling so that words will not have to be laboriously sounded out. Fluency with the elements will build fluency with sentences and passages. The process of sounding out is a first step that builds the essential foundation for differentiating, remembering, and quickly recognizing words in print. As word recognition is mastered, cognitive "desk space" is freed up for higher-level comprehension.

Consolidated Alphabetic Stage

Many children do not complete the transition to consolidated, accurate, and fluent reading and writing until second or third grade. Longer words, words with unusual spellings, and analysis of base words, endings, prefixes, compounds, contractions, and other constructions must be conquered. Vocabulary or word meaning knowledge is both enhanced by and dependent upon students' awareness of word structure, including meaningful parts (morphemes).

Children who have a good handle on the most regular sound-symbol elements may teach themselves about sound-symbol patterns from exposure to many examples. These are the "self-teachers" who pick up speed and insight about words as they store more and more examples of sound-spellings in memory. Children who are less able to compare words and figure out sound-symbol links will need continuing instruction in the entire sound–symbol correspondence system, especially for spelling. Nevertheless, most children benefit from systematic teaching of the code.

Brain Studies of Reading Growth

The brain illustrations in *Figure 4.6* (next page) are based on the results of studies of changes in eight children's brain–activation patterns as they responded to reading instruction (Simos et al., 2002). Before students learned the alphabetic code, they attempted to recognize words by shape or by one or two letters. Consistent with Ehri's (1996) conception of a prealphabetic reading phase, they did not activate their phonological processors while trying to read words. After two months of daily, systematic instruction in how to match symbols and sounds, note that other pathways were established to facilitate complete and accurate use of the alphabetic code, as measured by reading phonically regular nonsense words. New words were processed through these pathways, corresponding to the characteristics of Ehri's (1996) later alphabetic stage of reading.

Figure 4.6 How Activation Patterns in the Brain Change as Reading Is Learned

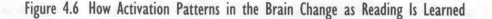

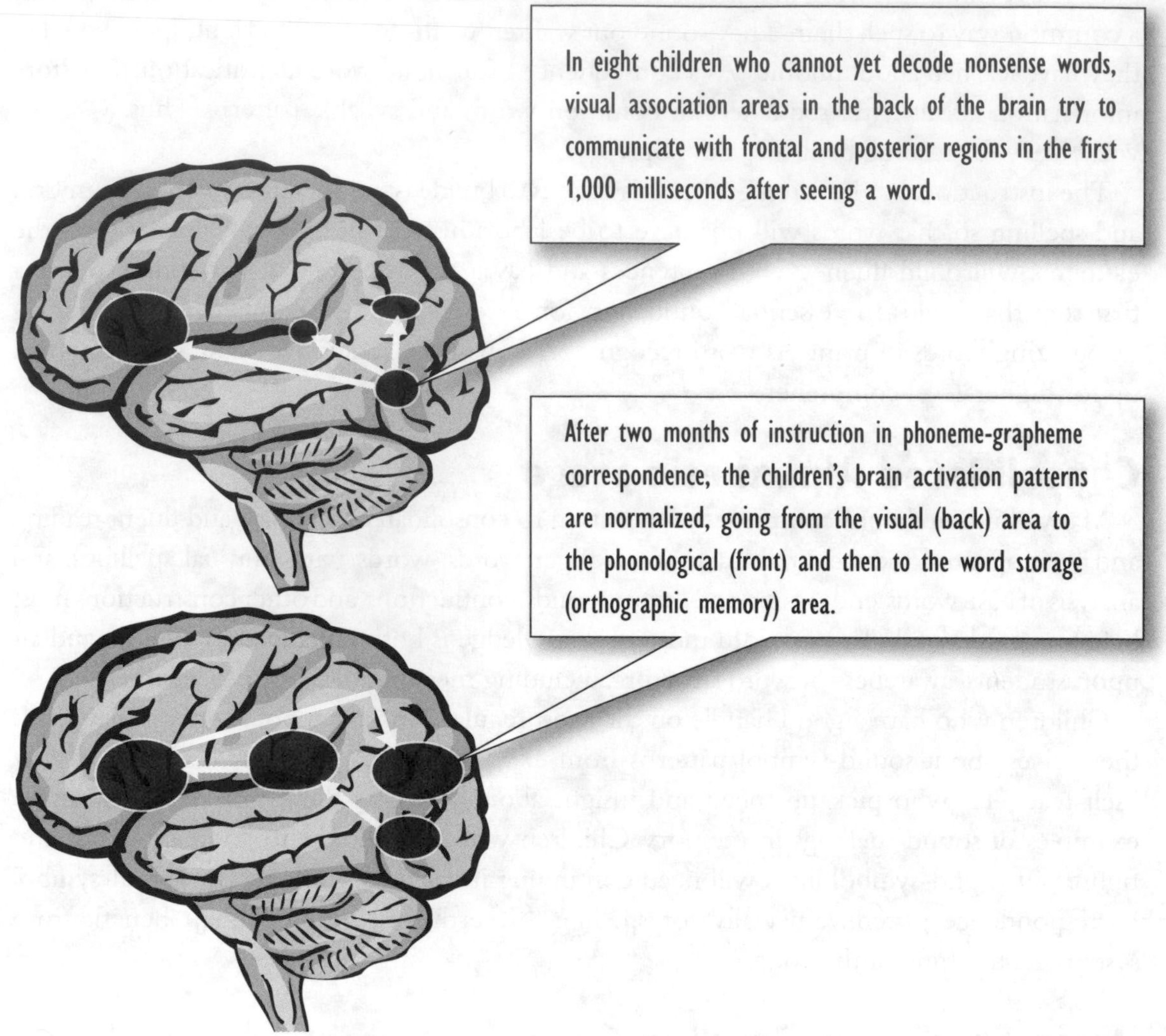

In eight children who cannot yet decode nonsense words, visual association areas in the back of the brain try to communicate with frontal and posterior regions in the first 1,000 milliseconds after seeing a word.

After two months of instruction in phoneme-grapheme correspondence, the children's brain activation patterns are normalized, going from the visual (back) area to the phonological (front) and then to the word storage (orthographic memory) area.

As decoding pathways were established, novice readers could decode new words accurately. This achievement enabled them to build a store of known words in orthographic memory that were then recognized quickly by sight. There were significant gains in word recognition and decoding in all eight cases in this study, and the resulting progression of brain activity resembled the profile typical of normally progressing young readers.

This experiment also found that a few of the children did not respond well to a few months of instruction and did not normalize the pathways involved in word recognition during the study. Those non-responders probably represent a small group of "treatment resistors," or those who would likely be eligible for special education and sustained, intensive remediation if the pattern continued.

Achieving Passage-Reading Fluency With Comprehension

In second and third grade, with decoding skills learned well enough to support word recognition accuracy and with daily reading practice, children usually consolidate their reading skills and build reading fluency. Their speed typically increases from about 60 words correct per minute (WCPM) at the end of first grade to about 120 WCPM in oral reading by the end of third grade. If this goal is not reached, reading may be too slow and inefficient to support sustained passage-reading comprehension. While many teachers believe that poor comprehension is the primary issue for poor readers, many of those students are still struggling with aspects of decoding accuracy and fluency and do not have the cognitive desk space available to think about their reading. As a result, many poor readers at this level may still need remediation at the decoding and/or fluency levels (Hamilton & Shinn, 2003). Speed and accuracy of oral passage reading in grades 1–3 predicts comprehension of passages on high-stakes examinations such as the Stanford Achievement Test.

Extensive reading in material that can be read with accuracy is the best way for children to develop fluency. Better readers read more and, by reading more, get to be even better readers. If children read too slowly, a number of instructional techniques may help them get up to speed. LETRS Module 5 addresses reading fluency in depth.

The sense of urgency that third-grade teachers feel about their students' skills stems from the reality that reading instruction often ends by fourth grade, and if students are not skilled by then, they will have few opportunities to make up lost ground. Fourth graders are expected to read independently, silently, and selectively, and teachers assume they have acquired the reading skills necessary to do so. Many students, however, need continuing instruction in decoding longer and less common words, vocabulary, text structure (especially expository text), regulation of reading speed according to the purpose of an assignment, monitoring comprehension, and comprehension skills such as asking the author questions, stating or writing summaries of main ideas, and understanding the organization of a text. LETRS Modules 4, 6, and 11 address the vocabulary and comprehension components of reading.

Scarborough's "Rope" Model of Reading Development

In actuality, skilled reading is attained when many subskills are automatized. Scarborough (2001) represented the achievement of fluency in both decoding and language comprehension with a rope image. Note that there are many more "threads" to add to the "reading rope" when language comprehension must be considered in addition to word recognition.

Figure 4.7 The Many Strands That Are Woven Into Skilled Reading
(Scarborough, 2001, p. 98)

LANGUAGE COMPREHENSION

BACKGROUND KNOWLEDGE
(facts, concepts, etc.)

VOCABULARY
(breadth, precision, links, etc.)

LANGUAGE STRUCTURES
(syntax, semantics, etc.)

VERBAL REASONING
(inference, metaphor, etc.)

LITERACY KNOWLEDGE
(print concepts, genres, etc.)

WORD RECOGNITION

PHONOLOGICAL AWARENESS
(syllables, phonemes, etc.)

DECODING (alphabetic principle,
spelling-sound correspondences)

SIGHT RECOGNITION
(of familiar words)

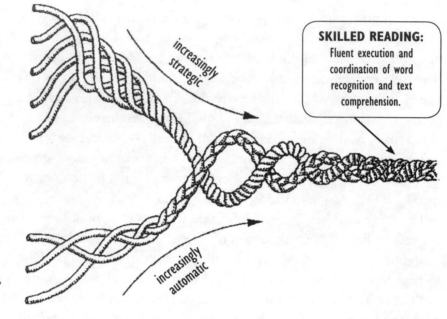

increasingly strategic

SKILLED READING:
Fluent execution and coordination of word recognition and text comprehension.

increasingly automatic

Used with permission of Hollis Scarborough.

Scarborough conceptualizes skilled reading as a combination of strands, or subskills, that interact with one another and that are increasingly amalgamated as reading skill is acquired. *Figure 4.7* shows clearly that fluent reading depends on automatic execution of both word recognition and comprehension subskills.

Exercise 4.2 Review Reading and Spelling Development With Writing Samples

• Revisit these writing samples from the Warm-Up activity. What more can you say about them after learning about reading and spelling development?

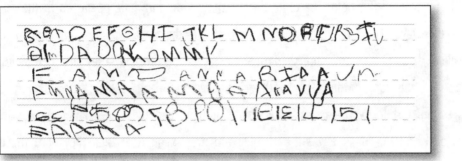

Student C: Writing sample, September

a wich toock the pretty pretty princess
ard shee brot the princess and thennti
wich toock the priness in to the cich
in   and the wich tide the princess
to a char and then a prince savd
her and then thae livd haplee evr
aftr

Student C: Writing sample, the following April

September writing sample:

_____

_____

_____

April writing sample:

_____

_____

_____

Exercise 4.2 (Alternative)
For Teachers of Older Students

- Read this composition that was written by a sixth-grade student, and then answer the questions below.

"TITEL WAVE!" But befor she could do eny thing a dig hug hole opend up in the middel of the wave. The two gerles started to run, but the wave was tow fast for them. It suked them in the hole and then they startet floping around, they hit ther hedes on part of the rocy botom. They both got knoked out dead. When they woke up they were in a room whith a deap blue ceiing and the bed they were laing on was made of orol and the blanket was a dark blue tint over them. Gust then they herd the dore creek open. A girl with really long brown hair and a white sooba biving shurt and pants with a "sbc" on the shurt. Walked over to them and said "hellou" my name is Maddie, wats your name." I'm mary and shes ruby mary said. "Well come with me and lets get some food."

1. Find examples of phonetic, sound-by-sound spellings. Which of Ehri's phases best describes this trait?

   _____

   _____

   _____

2. Which processing system—phonological or orthographic—appears to be more underdeveloped in this student? Why do you think so?

   _____

   _____

   _____

3. This student is a dysfluent reader. Why would you expect a sixth-grade student who spells phonetically to be a dysfluent reader? (If the student moved through this stage to the next stage of reading and spelling development, what would he have to learn to do?)

   _____

   _____

   _____

Five Essential Components of Comprehensive Reading Instruction

Where did the five essential components come from?

The federally funded Reading First program (No Child Left Behind Act, 2001) enumerated essential components of reading instruction, based on the Report of the National Reading Panel (NICHD, 2000). Commissioned by Congress, the National Reading Panel report was based on a meta-analysis, or comprehensive review and statistical synthesis, of scientific studies of effective reading instruction. Evidence was strong that the most effective instructional programs taught all of the components thoroughly and skillfully.

Since then, the five essential components of reading have served to organize programs of instruction, assessment programs, and teacher education requirements. These components are now found in all core, comprehensive reading programs by major publishers, and most states who are referring to "scientifically based reading instruction" in their regulations are referring to these components:

- Phonemic awareness and letter knowledge
- Phonics, decoding, spelling and word recognition
- Text reading fluency
- Vocabulary (knowledge of word meanings)
- Comprehension of connected text

Moreover, these additional components are often added to the list of essentials:

- Written expression
- Oral language (listening and speaking)
- Ongoing assessment

Familiarity with the five essential components and their treatment in core, comprehensive reading programs is imperative for all teachers of reading. Additional exercises are included in *Appendix C* for those who should spend more time learning to identify the components.

What should be emphasized at each stage of reading development?

Although all components of a comprehensive lesson are needed at all levels, different skills and activities will be emphasized at different stages of reading development (see *Table 4.3*, next page). At the prealphabetic stage, alphabet knowledge, phonological awareness, and language development deserve emphasis. In the early alphabetic and later alphabetic stages, phonological awareness and phonics, word recognition, and spelling should receive emphasis with daily practice reading simple, decodable books. Vocabulary and comprehension are taught from the beginning, with an early emphasis on reading aloud until children can read "real" books for themselves. Reading with fluency, expanding vocabulary, and deciphering longer words merit emphasis in second grade. Advanced phonics, including the study of meaningful word parts, should continue throughout elementary school.

Table 4.3 Reading Instruction Components Typically Emphasized at Each Grade Level

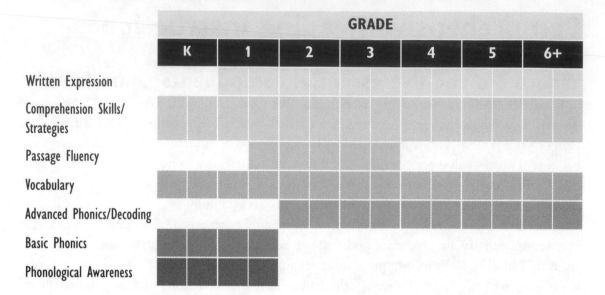

	GRADE						
	K	1	2	3	4	5	6+
Written Expression		■	■	■	■	■	■
Comprehension Skills/ Strategies	■	■	■	■	■	■	■
Passage Fluency		■	■	■	■	■	■
Vocabulary	■	■	■	■	■	■	■
Advanced Phonics/Decoding			■	■	■	■	■
Basic Phonics	■	■	■				
Phonological Awareness	■	■	■				

As children gain comfort and skill with written language, more instructional time will be devoted to comprehension at the word, sentence, and whole-text levels. Programs should promote wide reading in a variety of texts and thorough discussions of text meanings. Ultimately, the best readers are those who read the most and who learn to question deeply as they read. Written responses to reading promote that kind of deep reflection.

Finally, it is the interactions or interrelationships among the essential components that will receive the most attention in LETRS. Like any well-designed machine, the reading brain works best when the right parts are engaged in the right order and at the right speeds to accomplish specific jobs.

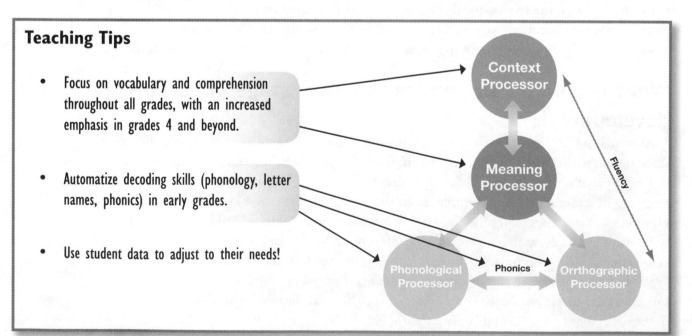

Teaching Tips

- Focus on vocabulary and comprehension throughout all grades, with an increased emphasis in grades 4 and beyond.

- Automatize decoding skills (phonology, letter names, phonics) in early grades.

- Use student data to adjust to their needs!

Context Processor

Meaning Processor

Phonological Processor

Phonics

Orrthographic Processor

Fluency

Chapter 5

Dyslexia and Other Causes of Reading Disability

Learner Objectives for Chapter 5

- Define dyslexia.
- Describe subtypes of reading disability.
- Understand how activation patterns in the brain change in response to instruction.

Warm-Up: Identify a Student With Reading Difficulties

- Using the frameworks we have presented, enumerate several possible causes for reading problems. Identify a student you have worked with who has or has had reading difficulties:
  - What was he/she like?
  - What appeared to be the reason(s) for his/her difficulties?
- Share your observations with a partner sitting next to you.

Reading Problems Have Many Causes

Genetic, environmental, and instructional factors all contribute to the growth of reading skill. Some children come to school without the kind of exposure to books, book language, and vocabulary that support the development of literacy. These children can be called "experience-deficient" and will be the focus of discussion in LETRS modules on vocabulary (Module 4) and oral language development (Module 6). Some students have generally weak verbal abilities in all areas. An increasing number of students are learning English as a second language. Some children fall behind, even though they are capable of learning, simply because their instruction has been insufficient. And some have legitimate, biologically based learning disabilities that deserve to be properly assessed, classified, and treated through remedial and special education.

What Is Dyslexia?

Dyslexia is a useful term for a specific, biologically based disorder that adversely affects the ability to read and write. Dyslexia ("difficulty with language" according to its Greek roots) is a common problem that can affect people of all IQ levels and all walks of life across a continuum of reading ability. You can be gifted and dyslexic, or a slow learner and dyslexic. Dyslexia does not refer to "making reversals" or "seeing things backwards." Estimates of the prevalence of intrinsic or biologically based reading disabilities vary from 17 percent in the Connecticut Longitudinal Study at Yale University (Shaywitz, 2003) to 11 percent in an epidemiological study by the Mayo Clinic in Rochester, Minnesota.

Dyslexia is currently defined by the International Dyslexia Association and the National Institutes of Child Health and Human Development as follows (Lyon, Shaywitz & Shaywitz, 2003):

> Dyslexia is a specific learning disability that is neurobiological in origin. It is characterized by difficulties with accurate and/or fluent word recognition and by poor spelling and decoding abilities. These difficulties typically result from a deficit in the phonological component of language that is often unexpected in relation to other cognitive abilities and the provision of effective classroom instruction. Secondary consequences may include problems in reading comprehension and reduced reading experience that can impede growth of vocabulary and background knowledge.

Subtypes of Reading Disability

Figure 5.1 Diagram of Subtypes of Reading Disability

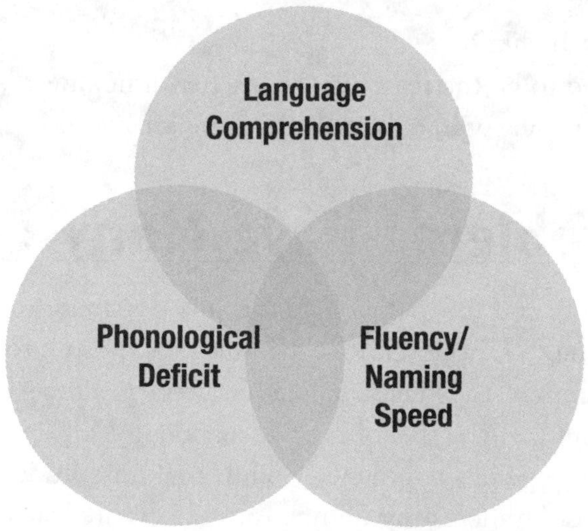

Researchers have made considerable progress in understanding all types of reading disabilities (Fletcher et al., 2007). For purposes of research, "reading impaired" children may be all those who score below the 30th percentile in basic reading skill. Among all of those poor readers, about 70–80 percent have trouble with accurate and fluent word recognition that originates with weaknesses in phonological processing, often in combination with fluency and comprehension problems. These students have obvious trouble learning sound-symbol correspondence, sounding out words, and spelling. The term *dyslexic* is most often applied to this group.

Another 10–15 percent of poor readers appear to be accurate but too slow in word recognition and text reading. They have specific weaknesses with *speed* of word recognition and automatic recall of word spellings, although they do relatively well on tests of phoneme awareness and other phonological skills. They have trouble developing automatic recognition of words by sight and tend to spell phonetically but not accurately. This subgroup is thought to have relative strengths in phonological processing, but the nature of their relative weakness is still debated by reading scientists (Fletcher et al, 2007; Katzir et al., 2006; Wolf & Bowers, 1999). Some argue that the problem is primarily one of timing or processing speed, and others propose that there is a specific deficit within the orthographic processor that affects the storage and recall of exact letter sequences. This processing speed/orthographic subgroup generally has milder difficulties with reading than students with phonological processing deficits.

Yet another 10–15 percent of poor readers appear to decode words better than they can comprehend the meanings of passages. These poor readers are distinguished from dyslexic poor readers because they can read words accurately and quickly and they can spell. Their problems are caused by disorders of social reasoning, abstract verbal reasoning, or language comprehension.

To summarize, researchers currently propose that there are three kinds of developmental reading disabilities that often overlap but that can be separate and distinct:

1. *Phonological deficit*, implicating a core problem in the phonological processing system of oral language.
2. *Processing speed/orthographic processing deficit*, affecting speed and accuracy of printed word recognition (also called *naming speed problem* or *fluency problem*).
3. *Comprehension deficit*, often coinciding with the first two types of problems, but specifically found in children with social-linguistic disabilities (e.g., autism spectrum), vocabulary weaknesses, generalized language learning disorders, and learning difficulties that affect abstract reasoning and logical thinking.

If a student has a prominent and specific weakness in *either* phonological or rapid print (naming-speed) processing, they are said to have a *single deficit* in word recognition. If they have a combination of phonological and naming-speed deficits, they are said to have a *double deficit* (Wolf & Bowers, 1999). Double-deficit children are more common than single-deficit and are also the most challenging to remediate. Related and coexisting problems in children with reading disabilities often include:

- faulty pencil grip and letter formation;
- attention problems;
- anxiety;
- task avoidance;
- weak impulse control;
- distractibility;
- problems with comprehension of spoken language; and
- confusion of mathematical signs and computation processes.

About 30 percent of all children with dyslexia also have attention deficit hyperactivity disorder (ADHD).

The Brain and Dyslexia

Figure 5.2 Brain Images Comparing 9-year-old Average Reader and
9-Year-Old Unremediated Poor Reader
(brain activation patterns recorded during nonsense word reading)
Image contributed and used with permission of Dr. Panagiotis Simos, University of Crete.

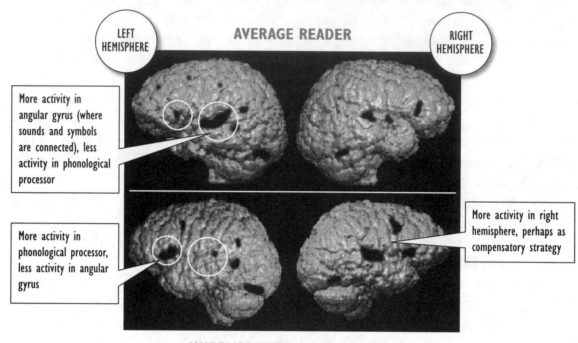

Figure 5.2 illustrates brain-activation profiles in two 9-year-old subjects. The top brain is that of a normally progressing child with no reading disability whose IQ is in the high-average range and whose basic reading skills on the Woodcock-Johnson test are at about the 75th percentile (high-average range). The bottom brain is that of another child of similar age and IQ with a severe reading disability. Activation patterns were recorded during a nonsense word reading task. Notice reduced activity in the left superior temporal gyrus and somewhat increased activity in frontal regions and right temporal regions in the child with a reading disability.

Several studies have now shown that dyslexic students' brain activation patterns can be "normalized" if remediation is early, intensive, and effectively designed (Blachman et al., 2004; Simos et al., 2007). The images in *Figure 5.3* show the effect of remediation on brain activation patterns during nonsense word reading for an 8-year-old subject with an IQ slightly above average and phonic decoding at the 9th percentile before remediation. After two months of intensive intervention on phoneme awareness, phonic decoding, and word recognition during reading, the child made significant gains in both word recognition and decoding. The child's basic reading skills improved to the 37th percentile. The lower set of images shows a corresponding increase in magnetic activity noted in the left temporal-parietal region.

Figure 5.3 Changes in Brain Activation Patterns in Response to Instruction (8-year-old poor reader who received remediation)

Image contributed and used with permission of Dr. Panagiotis Simos, University of Crete.

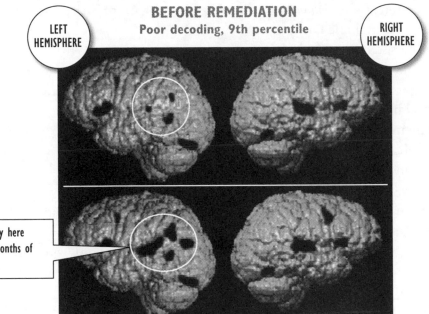

The School History of the Dyslexic Person

Although the definition of dyslexia represents scientific consensus, no two dyslexic individuals are exactly alike, and the manifestations of dyslexia change over time (Hudson, High, & Al Otaiba, 2007). The disorder can vary considerably from one individual to the next according to the:

- severity of the problem;
- duration of the problem;
- responsiveness of the problem to treatment or remediation;
- relative difficulty a person has with related aspects of reading, spelling, writing, math, or language learning;
- coexisting conditions, or existence of other types of problems with dyslexia, such as anxiety, attention, or word-retrieval difficulties; and
- coexisting strengths, or areas of talent and interest that enable a person to do well in life, such as visual-spatial , athletic, or intellectual gifts.

The following lists of "typical" symptoms at each grade level are given as a guide to understanding dyslexia, with the caution that any given individual might vary from what is typical.

- **Preschool: Getting Reading to Read**
  - Is late in learning to talk.
  - Is slow to learn new words.
  - Mixes up pronunciations of words much more or much longer than other children (e.g., says *aminal* for **animal**, *spusgetti* for **spaghetti**, *emeny* for **enemy**) even after multiple corrections.
  - Has persistent trouble with difficult speech sounds, such as /th/, /r/, /l/, and /w/.
  - May not enjoy looking at or following print in books when read aloud.

- **Kindergarten and First Grade: Beginning Reading Instruction**
  The child has trouble:
  - Remembering names of letters and recalling them quickly.
  - Recalling sounds that letters represent.
  - Breaking a simple word such as **zoo** or **cheese** into its separate speech sounds (i.e., /z/ /ū/; /ch/ /ē/ /z/).
  - Learning to recognize common words (e.g., family names, common labels, the most common words used in writing) by sight, or automatically.
  - Spelling sounds of words in a plausible way so that the words can be recognized by the reader.

- **Second and Third Grade**
  - Is unable to recognize important and common words by sight, or instantly, without having to laboriously sound them out.
  - Falters during the sounding out or letter-sound association (decoding) process, and recalls the wrong sounds for the letters and letter patterns.
  - Is a poor speller, with speech sounds omitted, wrong letters for sounds used, and poor recall for even the most common "little" words (e.g., **when**, **went**, **they**, **their**, **been**, **to**, **does**, **said**, **what**).
  - Reads too slowly and lacks appropriate expression, marked by many decoding or word recognition errors.
  - Loses the gist or meaning of the passage when reading is slow and/or inaccurate.
  - Guesses at unknown words on the basis of pictures, story theme, or one or two letters in a word.
  - Has inordinate difficulty with writing or completing written work.

- **Transition to "Reading to Learn"**
  - Is easily overwhelmed by reading and writing demands.
  - Misreads directions or word problems.
  - Struggles to keep up, taking unfinished classwork home in addition to regular homework.
  - Remains a poor speller and struggles to produce written work.

- **Intermediate (Fourth to Sixth) Grades**
  - Needs extra time on timed oral reading tests.
  - Will typically do poorly when asked to read lists of single, common words that are taken out of the context.
  - Spelling remains poor.
  - Appears to have a comprehension problem on a reading test, but when comprehension is measured through tests that do not require reading, it is often much better than the reading test would suggest.
  - May avoid reading and writing at all costs.
- **Middle School and High School**
  - May quickly fall apart in this new context.
  - The volume of work required, the amount of self-direction required, and demands on time and space management may all exceed the student's coping skills.
  - Needs note-taking skills, notebook organization, schedule compliance and time management, independent study habits, homework completion, and strategies for dealing with a slow reading rate.
  - Needs technology supports.
  - Needs accommodations on high-stakes testing (e.g., state proficiency tests, testing for the college admission process).

Exercise 5.1 | Three Second-Grade Children With Three Kinds of Reading Problems

SAMPLE 1

1.	bed	siup.	daf	bed
				ship
				drive
2.	bap			bump
3.	wine			when
4.	teran			train
5.	clost			closet
6.	cane			chase
7.	flot			float
8.	begs			beaches
9.	peroego			preparing
10.	pare			popping
11.	cart			cattle

Sample 1: Phonological processing and fluency (orthographic) weaknesses. On a November oral reading fluency test, this second-grader read slowly for her grade, about 55 WCPM. She stopped and guessed at words she didn't know when she read aloud. She misread simple words with short vowel sounds that most children know by early first grade. Her spelling test suggested that she was not aware of all the speech sounds in the dictated words and that she needed more instruction in phoneme awareness and phonics to build her accuracy in word reading.

1. Find two words in which the student left out consonant sounds.

    _____

2. Find two words that have digraphs (e.g., **wh, ch, sh, th**) but are not spelled with them.

    _____

Exercise 5.1   (continued)

3. Find the word that the student spelled /v/ with the letter **f**. Why might a student confuse these two sounds?

    _____

4. Find two words in which short vowels are misspelled.

    _____

5. Find two words with more than one syllable. Can the student represent syllables in longer words?

    _____

SAMPLE 2

goo	(go)
ann	(and)
yel	(will)
hme	(him)
coc	(cook)
lot	(light)
jrs	(dress)
reh	(reach)
ntr	(enter)

Sample 2: Orthographic memory weakness and very slow reading (fluency or rate deficit). This second-grader read at about 40 WCPM at the end of second grade after she had practiced a passage several times. She was very slow. She sounded out each word as if she had not seen it before. Her spelling, however, was phonetically accurate. Most sounds in the dictated words were represented, some with letters whose names have the target sound. She "hears" the phonemes in one-syllable words but does not remember or recall the correct symbols for those sounds.

(continued)

Exercise 5.1   (continued)

1. Find the letter that this student uses for the /w/ sound. Why did she choose that letter?

    _____

2. Find the letter she uses for the /ch/ sound. Why did she choose that letter?

    _____

3. What does she think is the first sound in the word **dress**? Does that seem like a logical choice?

    _____

4. How does she spell long-vowel sounds?

    _____

SAMPLE 3

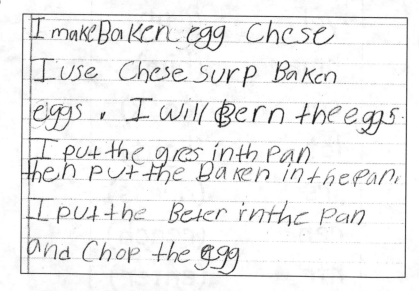

Sample 3: Language comprehension and production difficulty. At the end of second grade, this student was asked to write a description about how he would make breakfast for a friend. This draft was produced in 30 minutes. The class participated in brainstorming ideas before they wrote their drafts.

Exercise 5.1 (continued)

1. What is the strength of this student's composition?

   _____

2. What kinds of words are missing from the sentences?

   _____

3. Do you think he wrote fluently, or slowly and laboriously? Why?

   _____

   _____

4. Are the spellings mostly accurate phonetically? Is that a good sign?

   _____

Implications for Assessment

The frameworks that explain reading components, reading development, and reading difficulties that we have examined so far provide a template for understanding assessment. Each of the stages in Ehri's (1996) model and each of the strands in Scarborough's (2001) "reading rope" points to specific skills that students should accomplish before they can consolidate component skills in fluent reading. Studies that have focused on the prediction of later reading ability from the assessment of early reading skills (e.g., Good, Simmons, & Kame'enui, 2001; Scarborough, 2001; Torgesen, 2002) support the importance of sampling the following skills as children develop:

- **Prealphabetic phase**: Letter naming; initial sound isolation; concepts of print; vocabulary and oral language.
- **Early alphabetic phase**: Rapid automatic (timed) letter-naming (RAN); phoneme blending; phoneme segmentation; reading simple nonsense syllables; phonetic spelling accuracy; vocabulary and listening comprehension.
- **Later alphabetic phase**: Reading nonsense words; reading real words in lists; reading simple sentences and passages; phonetic spelling and real-word spelling; sound-symbol matching or knowledge of phonic elements; vocabulary; retelling of passages.
- **Consolidated alphabetic phase**: Silent passage reading with comprehension component; oral passage reading fluency; maze passage reading; real-word spelling.

Exercise 5.2 | DIBELS and the Four Processors

- Whether or not you use the *Dynamic Indicators of Basic Early Literacy Skills, 7th Edition* (DIBELS Next) (Good & Kaminski, 2010), place its subtests within the Four-Part Processing model of reading.

- Follow your instructor and use the diagram below to show which processing systems are sampled by each subtest.

- If appropriate, repeat this exercise as you analyze the content of another screening or diagnostic assessment that you are very familiar with.

DIBELS subtests:

First Sound Fluency (FSF)

Letter Naming Fluency (LNF)

Phoneme Segmentation Fluency (PSF)

Nonsense Word Fluency (NWF)

Oral Reading Fluency with Retell (DORF)

Word Use Fluency (WUF)

Daze Passages

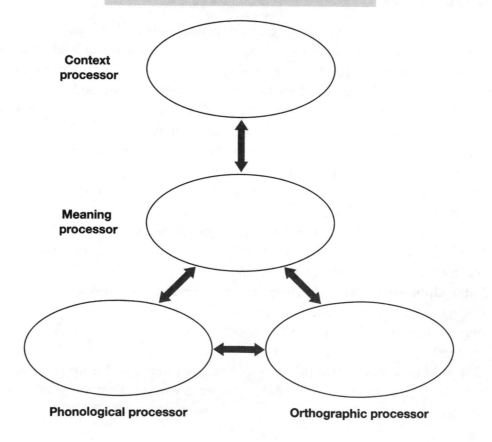

Context processor

Meaning processor

Phonological processor   Orthographic processor

Take 2 Review

- Complete this two-column organizer.
- In the first column are restatements of main ideas. Work with the group or your partner to complete the second column. List a few details that elaborate the main ideas or that state the relevance of those ideas for your school or classroom.

Knowledge/Main Ideas	Application/Details
1. Poor readers do not share the same type of reading disability; at least three subtypes are established in research.	
2. A glitch in one or more processing systems may cause a reading problem.	
3. The dyslexic brain may respond well to instruction.	

6 The Research Base for Understanding Reading

Learner Objectives for Chapter 6
- Know the characteristics of scientifically conducted reading research.
- Identify trustworthy sources for research reviews.
- Understand the meaning of "effect size" in intervention research.
- Survey evidence that teaching makes a difference in student outcomes.

Warm-Up: List Your Favorite Resources
- List the sources you depend on to guide your decisions about best practices in assessment and instruction.

_____

_____

_____

_____

_____

Why Bother With Scientific Research?

In our information-rich world, we have ready access to publications, Internet blogs, informational Web sites, radio, and television. Like most other professionals, educators are bombarded with opinions, philosophies, rhetoric, anecdotes, and assertions about instructional programs, materials, and methods. Sorting credible information from unsupported or unhelpful ideas can be difficult, especially when teachers are not trained in critical analysis of research. Not everything in writing is credible or equal in its value! This makes it difficult for teachers to sort through to find best practices for their students.

Nevertheless, teachers must solve many instructional problems every day. To do so, they may informally employ the scientific method. They observe and develop hunches, assess student learning, try out practices, and decide whether to stick with or change an approach, depending on the outcome. The elements of experimentation by thoughtful teachers, including observation, hypothesis-generation, planned implementation of lessons, measurement of results, and evaluation of the best way(s) to proceed, are realized in classroom research. "Researchers and educators are kindred spirits in their approach to knowledge, an important fact that can be used to forge a coalition to bring hard-won research knowledge to light in the classroom" (Stanovich & Stanovich, 2003, p. 35).

Classroom research will help guide instruction and classroom management, but the mark of a profession is that its members share common knowledge of proven, best practices. In the area of reading instruction, truths have been established (e.g., Adams, 1990; Anderson, Heibert, Scott, & Wilkinson, 1985; McCardle & Chhabra, 2004; Rayner et al, 2001; Snow, Burns, & Griffin, 1998). Relying on every teacher to reinvent these truths through experimentation is impractical and irresponsible. The question we should always ask of ourselves and our students is, "If I do *something else* in my teaching, will I get a *better* result with my class? With certain students? In a certain skill area?" Scientifically conducted research can provide answers (or at least guidance) to many questions about what is best to do, with whom, and at what point in reading development. Research can also enable us to get the biggest return on the investment of tax dollars that support education.

What Is Scientific Research?

A definition of scientifically based research was embedded in the federally funded Reading First program (Fletcher & Francis, 2004; Sweet, 2004). Standards have also been set by the What Works Clearinghouse of the Institute for Education Sciences (http://ies.ed.gov/ncee/wwc/). Research standards have driven the process by which grants are awarded through the National Institutes of Health (Lyon & Moats, 1997). Standards are supported as well by the editorial policies of many professional journals that publish research reports only if they meet stringent scientific criteria. To meet scientific standards, studies must:

1. Employ systematic, empirical methods that draw on observation and/or experiment;

2. Involve rigorous data analyses that are adequate to test the stated hypotheses and justify the general conclusions;

3. Rely on measurements or observational methods that provide valid data across evaluators and observers, and across multiple measurements and observations; and

4. Be accepted by a peer-reviewed journal or approved by a panel of independent experts through a comparatively rigorous, objective, and scientific review.

Hypotheses for study are usually generated on the basis of a thorough review of what is already known and proven about a question. **Systematic, empirical** methods of investigation may include qualitative and/or quantitative data-gathering and analysis. **Qualitative** methods include such tools as observations, checklists, rating scales, interviews, and self-reports. **Quantitative** methods rely on numerical or statistical measurement. Methods, moreover, should fit the hypothesis that is being tested. Systematic data-gathering is accomplished as objectively as possible, and the reliability of observations is established through various means.

Exercise 6.1 | Qualitative and Quantitative Research

• Follow your presenter as you explore the differences between *qualitative* and *quantitative* research.

Rigorous data analyses are designed to minimize experimenter bias and are usually planned before an experiment is conducted. A rigorous analysis is designed to uncover all the reasons why a particular result might have been obtained (and all the reasons why it might not have been obtained). Conclusions drawn from the study should not be overstated or over-generalized. Results from any study can be generalized only to students *who are like those in the study*. Thus, it is very important for experimenters to define and to report the relevant characteristics of the students they have included in their experiment.

Results of rigorous studies of reading and literacy instruction should be measured and reported with multiple outcome measures. No one measure is satisfactory because it may be unreliable or may measure only one aspect of reading or writing. Some rigorous studies conducted over a year or more will use multiple measures of student growth several times over the course of the study. Using only a pretest and posttest may obscure interesting features of students' response to instruction.

Peer-reviewed journal articles are far more important in defining the truths we seek than opinion pieces, arguments promoted by individuals with strong beliefs, or anecdotal reports of what has worked in one classroom. The process of peer review is conducted "blind"; that is, without the reviewers knowing the author(s) of a study and without the author(s) of the study knowing who reviewed their work. Reviewers are selected because they are experts on the topic at hand. Peer review also occurs during meta-analyses or independent reviews of selected works by an agency or commission. As the National Reading Panel (NICHD, 2000) documented, there are many more publications about reading and reading instruction that are *not* scientifically conducted and peer-reviewed than there are peer-reviewed, rigorous scientific studies. Some nonscientific publications contain excellent critiques, summaries, and explorations of issues that add great value to the field, but they should not be mistaken for scientific journals.

Examples of Scientific Journals	Examples of Practitioner Journals, Policy Papers, and Other Nonscientific Publications
Annals of Dyslexia	*The Reading Teacher*
Journal of Learning Disabilities	*Intervention in the Schools*
Journal of Educational Psychology	*American Educator*
Reading Research Quarterly	*Educational Leadership*
Reading and Writing: An Interdisciplinary Journal	*Phi Delta Kappan*
Child Development	*Perspectives on Language and Literacy*
American Educational Research Journal	*Every Child Reading: A Professional Development Guide*
Scientific Studies of Reading	*National School Boards Association Journal*

(continued)

Exercise 6.1 (continued)

Repeating, or the replication of, a finding or claim is an important part of scientific work. Replication is possible only if scientists have described their work in such detail and with such accuracy that another team of investigators could repeat the study if they wished to do so. If a research finding is replicated or confirmed by other scientists, its findings are more likely to be true. When researchers seek to replicate the findings of other researchers, they usually use somewhat different study designs or methods and seek to remedy any problems evident in earlier studies. Each study's findings contribute a piece of the overall solution to the research question or problem. Answers to important issues in education are usually obtained with a series of studies that build on one another. Replication helps answer the question, "If one study shows student improvement in reading, can we do the same approach in other geographic areas or with other populations and get similar results?"

Scientific endeavor proceeds in stages. Hypotheses usually arise from ideas and observations about phenomena that then need to be more formally tested. Case studies, such as those done in single classrooms or those done with a handful of children, help researchers refine their hypotheses. Case studies, however, are not sufficient for: (a) determining cause and effect; (b) comparing approaches to treatment or instruction; or (c) building theories that can explain results. What seems to work in your classroom will not necessarily work in another classroom and might not give you the "biggest bang for your buck." Larger-scale, controlled comparisons are necessary for that purpose.

Correlational studies can show that one variable predicts another or that two or more variables are related. For example, if the researcher expects that spelling and reading are interdependent, then the researcher can look for evidence that the reading and spelling scores of a group of well-defined individuals tend to predict one another. But if the researcher wants to know whether teaching reading will cause significant gains in spelling, the best strategy for investigating that question is to design a randomized, controlled experiment.

Longitudinal and cross-sectional studies. Longitudinal studies select a group of students and follow their progress over a long period of time. Cross-sectional studies occur at one point in time but sample students' performance across different ages or grade levels. In studies of reading education, a "long time" usually means two years or more. Longitudinal research is important because any aspect of instruction or intervention that is studied may have a short-term effect that disappears in a few months. For example, if we want to know the effects of retaining poor readers in third grade, we should look down the road at whether those students drop out or stay in school at higher rates by age 16, and we should measure the long-term effects of the remediation provided during the repeated year. Longitudinal research on students is expensive and difficult for many reasons (Keogh, 2004), but it affords us the best information about reading development.

Exercise 6.1   (continued)

Randomized experiments, the most rigorous or "gold standard" research, assign subjects to one or more treatment groups and control groups by lottery. The researcher prescribes and controls the implementation of the treatment condition(s) and holds other conditions constant. For example, the researcher could randomly assign some students to a group that receives guided oral-reading instruction; to another group that receives phoneme-grapheme analysis and syllabication instruction; and yet another group that receives one-minute drills on speed and accuracy of word recognition. The effect of these treatments on the outcome, or dependent, variable—spelling achievement—would be measured.

The outcome of such an experiment is typically reported as an **effect size** (sometimes abbreviated as **ES** or **f**). Effect size is a statistic that describes the results of an individual experiment or that can be used to evaluate the trends or results of a group of experiments that all pertain to the same research question. When the combined results of a series of studies are evaluated, the exercise is called a **meta-analysis**. For example, the Report of the National Reading Panel (NICHD, 2000) was a report of meta-analyses of several hundred existing studies on components of reading instruction. An **effect** is the change in student achievement that is presumably caused by the treatment, program, or method. Effect size expresses the magnitude of change in standard deviation units.

Exercise 6.2 | Understanding Effect Size

- Follow your presenter as you discover the importance of effect size in reading research:

   — Imagine that there is a line on the floor on one side of the room that represents the continuum of shoe size in the population, from very small to very large. Arrange yourselves on the continuum by your shoe size. (There should be a larger group in the middle, where the average sizes are, and smaller numbers of people on either end of the line.)

   — Follow your presenter as you act out effect sizes for various reading research results.

   — Mild or small effect sizes range from .2 to .4 standard deviations; moderate effect sizes range from .5 to .7 standard deviations; and major or strong effects are in the range of .8 standard deviations or greater.

Figure 6.1 Normal Curve With Standard Deviations and Percentages

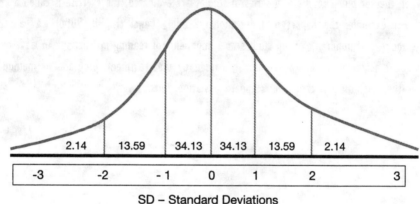

| 2.14 | 13.59 | 34.13 | 34.13 | 13.59 | 2.14 |

| -3 | -2 | -1 | 0 | 1 | 2 | 3 |

SD – Standard Deviations

After the findings of research on a particular issue have been replicated several or many times, scientists often arrive at a **consensus**. Experts come to agree, either formally or informally, that the evidence supports a theory or practice. Periodically, groups of experts are assembled by leading organizations such as the National Academy of Sciences, the American Educational Research Association, the Institute of Education Sciences, the Society for the Scientific Study of Reading, the American Psychological Association, or the National Institutes of Health to assess and report on scientific consensus. A professional educator who is a conscientious consumer of research can rely on the reports of these institutions to keep informed.

Exercise 6.3 | Shared Reading of a Research Article

• Complete the following grid as you participate in the shared reading of a research article.

Title:

Date:	Is this recent? ☐ Yes ☐ No
Author(s):	Do you know of the author(s)? ☐ Yes ☐ No
	Author(s)' theoretical backgrounds? Past research efforts?
Read Abstract (first page)	How many subjects?
	Ages?
	Grade levels?
	Good/poor readers?
	Question this study is trying to answer (hypothesis):
Read Summary (end of article)	Is the question posed in this study answered by the research?
	Can this research inform your teaching practice? If so, how? If not, why not?

(continued)

Exercise 6.3 (continued)

On Your Own

- Take two-column notes on this research article using the format below.
- Read, then reread the article to flesh out the salient points. Your presenter may direct you to complete this exercise and bring it to your next meeting.

	Big Ideas	Details
Abstract		
Discussion		
Summary / Conclusion		
Implications for your instruction		

Exercise 6.4   Module 1 Review: Match It!

• Work with your instructor to review these topics and vocabulary terms in Module 1.

• Write the definitions or explanations on the lines provided.

1. Definition of *dyslexia*: _____

_____

2. Most cited researcher on phases of word reading: _____

_____

3. Percentage of oral languages that have invented a writing system: _____

_____

4. Phonological processor: _____

_____

5. Orthographic processor: _____

_____

6. Semantic (Meaning) processor: _____

_____

7. Fluency: _____

_____

8. Double deficit: _____

_____

9. Undifferentiated poor reader: _____

_____

(continued)

Exercise 6.4 (continued)

10. Early Alphabetic phase: _____

_____

11. Quantitative research: _____

_____

12. NRP: _____

_____

13. Percentage of the adult U.S. population that reads poorly: _____

_____

14. Morphophonemic: _____

_____

15. Phonics: _____

_____

16. Prealphabetic (Logographic) phase: _____

_____

17. Shallow orthography: _____

_____

Chapter 7
Leadership to Improve Reading and Language Skills

Learner Objectives for Chapter 7
- Enumerate the characteristics of successful reading initiatives.
- Understand why intensive effort is necessary.
- Contrast a Response to Intervention (RtI) approach with a discrepancy model for identifying students who need special education.
- Outline the practices of a "multitiered" approach to organizing reading instruction schoolwide.

Warm-Up
- Share with another participant what your state, district, or school has been doing to improve reading outcomes in the elementary school population. What is the time frame for these initiatives?

What Successful Schools Do

The Florida Center for Reading Research recently issued a summary of the characteristics of Reading First schools that were beating the odds in the 2005–2006 school year (Crawford & Torgesen, 2006). Ten schools whose students' rate of growth exceeded those of schools with similar populations demonstrated these seven common characteristics:
- Strong leadership;
- Positive belief and teacher dedication;
- Data utilization and analysis;
- Effective scheduling;
- Professional development;
- Scientifically based intervention programs; and
- Parent involvement.

We will consider how each of these qualities may be cultivated but will emphasize the importance of a common knowledge base that drives practices in assessment and instruction.

The Purpose of Leadership

Studies of successful school improvement inevitably find that results hinge on strong, effective leadership (Chenowith, 2007; Denton, Foorman, & Mathes, 2003; Elmore, 2004). Leadership that engenders reading achievement and academic results requires an informed and consistent focus on instructional practices and teacher performance. Improvement of instruction, in turn, requires continuous learning on everyone's part. Mandates to improve test scores or implement specific programs are not sufficient to build capacity or expertise. As Elmore (2004, p. 69) states:

> My authority to require you to do something you might not otherwise do depends on my capacity to create the opportunity for you to learn how to do it, and to educate me on the process of learning how to do it, so that I become better at enabling you to do it the next time.

An instructional leader establishes goals and creates a context in which those goals can be achieved through mutual and reciprocal learning. Goals should be driven by student data that is *interpreted within research-based conceptual models* that everyone shares and understands. Some of our studies have shown, for example, that teachers without sufficient training in the underlying concepts of early screening instruments and progress-monitoring tools do not use the data to inform instruction, even if they are mandated to do so (Roehrig, Duggar, Moats, Glover, & Mincey, in press). If a faculty is divided by differences in philosophy, methodology, or interpretive framework, then productive teamwork is nearly impossible. Shared knowledge of reading development, reading difficulties, and best practices supported by research enables a faculty to move forward as a learning community. In the first part of this module, and in subsequent modules of LETRS, we teach the pivotal concepts and information that can help unify a faculty team as follows:

- The roles that four major language-processing systems play in reading development.
- The stages of reading development.
- The relationship between oral-language and written-language learning.
- The components of research-based instruction.
- The changing relationship among those components over time.
- The nature of systematic, explicit teaching.

Within each of these conceptual frameworks are many specific facts, principles, interpretive skills, and teaching behaviors to be learned. But as mastery of those bedrock concepts is acquired, practices that are often embedded in core, comprehensive programs or that are mandated in district policies or that are reflected in district or state standards begin to make sense. Teachers are much more likely to try new techniques or programs when the reasons for doing so are understood. Positive belief and teacher dedication are engendered when teachers are confident that they know what to do and why they are doing it.

A Reality: Reading Problems Are Resistant to Change

Changing reading achievement in a school system can be very hard work because reading talent is distributed on a normal curve, and a good portion of student populations are not wired up to process printed symbols accurately or efficiently. All of us are affected by our "reading genes," and some of us were given more talent than others when it comes to processing written language (Olson, 2004). In addition, vast differences in home experience and opportunities to learn affect our school population, and individuals bring different levels of language and verbal reasoning ability to the task of reading. The best predictor, for any child, of later reading achievement is where the child starts out on early indicators of basic reading skill (Mehta et al., 2005). The correlation between initial reading achievement and later reading achievement is very high, between .83 and .90. To propose that most children can learn to read, at least at basic levels, implies that the instruction must be informed enough and intensive enough to beat the odds or to defy prediction.

Initial reading achievement also starts a self-fulfilling cycle of reading growth that plays out through the grades. As Anderson, Wilson, and Fielding (1988) once calculated, children who read poorly read a lot less on their own than children who read well. A fifth-grader who functions at the 30th percentile typically reads independently for less than two minutes per day, whereas a child at the 70th percentile reads for an average of ten minutes per day. Over the year, the better reader has probably read at least 600,000 words, while the poorer reader has read a mere 100,000 words. A voracious reader (at the high end of the scale) may read up to 4 million words over a year's time, while the reading-disabled child reads hardly at all. These differences in practice and exposure to vocabulary and academic language have enormous impacts on overall reading growth.

When we face the implications of these data full-on, it should not surprise us that:

- Reading initiatives require whole-school involvement and systemic planning (King & Torgesen, 2006; Denton et al., 2003).
- Reading initiatives often take three to five years to achieve full benefit (King & Torgesen, 2006).
- Intensive work is required. To meet the needs of all children, 2.5 to 3 hours per day may be needed for reading, language, and writing instruction.
- Many children will beat the odds, but some will remain poor readers, even with the best instruction, and will need accommodations and modifications of assessments, standards and curriculum.
- Instruction must be differentiated, as children will never progress at a uniform rate.

Data Utilization and Analysis

All decisions about resource allocation, instructional programs, scheduling, and grouping of students should be based on multiple sources of data. These may include:

- screening assessments (e.g., DIBELS® [Good & Kaminski, 2005]; AIMSweb®, Web site: http://www.aimsweb.com; Children's Progress Assessments, Web site: http://www.childrensprogress.com/page1-82.htm), usually three times per school year;
- progress monitoring (e.g., DIBELS Oral Reading Fluency) as needed, on a frequent basis;
- end-of-year achievement tests;
- unit tests; and
- informal diagnostic surveys.

Teachers' schedules must allow for bimonthly or monthly data-analysis meetings. These meetings should be structured for specific outcomes, such as rearrangement of student groupings or implementation of instructional changes. Some schools use a late-start morning or an early-dismissal day to make time for these meetings.

Response to Intervention (RtI) and Tiered Instructional Models

In addition to an emphasis on early identification and prevention of reading problems, Reading First and other federal and state initiatives have also promoted a "tiered" approach to reading instruction in schools (Fuchs & Fuchs, 2006; The University of Texas, 2005). The purpose of the RtI provision in federal law governing eligibility for special education is to encourage states and districts to move beyond the discrepancy model for determining if a student has a learning disability. A discrepancy criterion has required students to demonstrate a wide difference between their IQ scores and their achievement scores on standardized testing in order to be classified as having a learning disability.

The RtI approach is also used more generally to provide services for all at-risk students, *before* they fall behind or are referred to special education for help. This process implies that: (a) all students will be screened periodically; (b) regular classroom instruction will be very effective; (c) a continuum of supplementary interventions will be used, according to student need; and (d) students will receive small-group instruction. The concept of a tiered approach to the organization and delivery of instruction is now used to describe how an entire school can organize its program of assessment and instruction. It emphasizes the importance of systemic alignment of programs and practices, a common knowledge base for all teachers, and continual teamwork. In the Texas model, the tiers are characterized as follows:

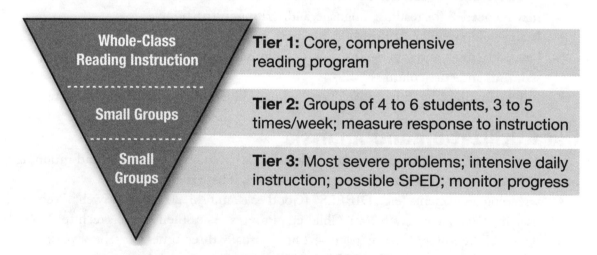

- **Tier 1**: *Regular classroom instruction with a core, comprehensive program.* If teaching with the program is effective and the program is a good match for students in the class, 70–80 percent of the students should make adequate progress toward grade-level standards, especially if in-class instructional groupings are used effectively.

- **Tier 2**: *Supplemental, small-group instruction, typically four to six students in a group, that meets three to five times per week.* Small-group supplemental instruction is particularly important for students who are in the "strategic" or "mildly at risk" range. Between 15 and 30 percent of students typically need Tier 2 instruction, which focuses on the components and skills most important for increasing student progress in the core, comprehensive program. Progress toward specific learning goals is monitored frequently.

- **Tier 3**: *Intensive intervention or remediation for 5–15 percent of students with the most severe difficulties with reading and writing.* These students typically require daily instruction, programs specifically designed for moderate to severe learning difficulties, the services of trained reading intervention specialists, and very small groups (i.e., two to three students) with similar needs.

A tiered model of instruction and intervention is recommended for schools that wish to move beyond a discrepancy and "wait to fail" approach to special education and remedial services (National Association of State Directors of Special Education [NASDSE], 2006). The focus of RtI is on instruction and results. Grade retentions are reduced because interventions—beginning in kindergarten—are ongoing, and the entire system relies less on special education services as the solution for children who are more difficult to teach.

The success of RtI in reducing reading failure will depend on the availability of quality instruction delivered by well-trained teachers, and also on meaningful use of progress-monitoring, screening, and diagnostic assessments to determine how instruction needs to be adjusted. These conditions, in turn, cannot be created without a substantial commitment to professional development.

Scientifically Based Classroom Programs

Is there one best program for K–grade 3 reading instruction in the regular classroom? Comparative studies of core, comprehensive programs are few (e.g., Foorman, Francis, Fletcher, Schatschneider, & Mehta, 1998). Even if expensive and complex comparative studies on programs were to be conducted, publishers regularly change their products, and study results may be obsolete within months. Our NICHD Early Interventions Project, which involved 17 schools, used four different reading programs: the 1995–1998 versions of Open Court Reading (SRA/McGraw-Hill), Houghton Mifflin Reading, Reading Mastery (McGraw-Hill), and Success for All. There were high-achieving and low-achieving classrooms in the schools that used each program. The overriding factors in accounting for classroom outcomes were: (a) the school context; (b) the fidelity of implementation of the chosen program, including time on-task; (c) the quality of the teacher; and (d) incoming skill levels of the student. A study that examined what successful schools in Texas were doing to achieve results showed that many different combinations of core programs and supplementary materials were associated with success (Denton, Vaughn, & Fletcher, 2003).

In comparison to individual teachers teaching however they like, the introduction of a structured, systematic, comprehensive classroom program used throughout a school and school system usually accounts for substantial schoolwide gains (EdSource, 2003). The adoption of one program allows for continuity and consistency across schools and within schools. Professional development on program implementation, however, must be relentless. Principals and coaches must support the implementation by using program-specific criteria for evaluating the fidelity of implementation. If the program includes all-important components, and quality implementation is emphasized, there is less chance that a major component will go untaught. Furthermore, many teachers learn the basics of how to teach reading by implementing a well-designed program.

How then would a school choose which program to purchase in the absence of evidence that one is superior to another? In addition to an examination of efficacy data from sites where the program is in use or any independent research studies that exist, one must do a careful analysis of a program's content and instructional design. Content is both information about selected topic areas and explicit instruction in language at *all* levels in parallel strands. A telling barometer of program quality is its instruction of phonology, spelling patterns, sentence structure, and word usage, because depth and sophistication in language are required to design these components well. Current programs are generally quite similar at the levels of vocabulary, classroom libraries, comprehension instruction, literature study, and composition. All programs, however, are imperfect, and their effectiveness depends largely on the knowledge and skill of the teacher using them.

The Use of Supplementary Programs and Materials

Approximately 15–30 percent of any class will require small-group support, even if the regular classroom program is efficacious and well taught. Quite a few programs and methodologies can be effective; research-based protocols vary in program balance, but all successful ones include explicit teaching of all essential strands (Mathes et al., 2005; Torgesen, Rashotte, & Alexander, 2001; Torgesen et al., 1999; Vellutino & Scanlon, 2002). Equally good results have been obtained at the first-grade level with a highly scripted approach that emphasizes word analysis and decodable text reading, and a "responsive" approach that emphasizes text reading and writing (Mathes et al., 2005). However, these supplementals are designed to intensify instruction in the critical skills necessary at various points in reading development and often provide more practice than core, comprehensive programs.

Optimal size for Tier 2 groups is generally three to six students (Vaughn & Linan-Thompson, 2003), although successful programs have varied in group size, duration of instruction, and frequency of instruction (Fletcher, Denton, Fuchs, & Vaughn, 2005). If student progress is carefully monitored at least once per month, and growth in an intervention is insufficient, the frequency, length, or methodology of instruction can be changed. These decisions require considerable expertise, however, and judgment about student response that allows for some students' slow rate of growth regardless of the method being used.

Intensive Intervention for Students With Severe Reading Disabilities

Students at this level are usually candidates for special education services, but not always. Some poor readers do not meet diagnostic criteria for a handicapping condition, especially if their problems are related to second-language learning or other complicating factors. Nevertheless, instruction may need to be more frequent and intense for them to progress and may need to involve the most expert teaching. Instruction at this level is generally given at a 1:1 or 1:3 ratio (not large groups) and occurs every day.

Programs validated on and designed for the poorest readers include a number of structured, systematic, multisensory, language-based interventions (Birsh, 2005). In addition, these programs employ carefully crafted instructional designs (Kame'enui, Carnine, Dixon, Simmons, & Coyne, 2002). The most effective programs balance basic decoding skills with vocabulary and text reading practice and are carried out systematically over a long period.

Beyond Grade 3: Teaching Older, Poor Readers

Approximately 70 percent of students identified as reading-disabled in the third grade continue to manifest reading difficulties through the end of high school (Shaywitz, 2003), even with resource room and consulting models of special education services. However, even older students can benefit from high-quality, intensive remedial interventions (Rashotte, MacPhee, & Torgesen, 2001; Swanson, Hoskyn, & Lee, 1999). Although less research exists about students beyond grade 3, many clinically validated models for instruction, both in the regular classroom and clinical settings, are established (Jetton & Dole, 2004).

Even if preventive screening and intervention programs are in place, and the number of students needing remediation is reduced within a school system, students will transfer into that system who are lacking in basic reading skill. These students should be screened immediately and assigned to intervention groups, if necessary. It is never too late to help older students with reading problems, but remediation can require up to two hours daily of intensive instruction in small groups (three to six students) for a year or two (Torgesen, Alexander, et al., 2001). The need for specialized remediation will not be circumvented with a strong preventive program. Even when successfully remediated, students who are treated after grade 1 often continue to be dysfluent readers. Accommodations of various kinds will continue to be necessary for students whose reading rates are very slow or who function below grade level in reading, language, and writing.

The practice of forced grade repetition for failing students has little justification from research and is likely to increase the probability of students dropping out of school (Jimerson, 2001).

Professional Development for Teachers

Successful implementation of a coordinated three-tier program requires a heavy dose of program-specific professional development, including: (a) courses to educate teachers about why they are doing what they are doing (LETRS!); (b) in-class coaching and mentoring; (c) video modeling; and (d) instructional leadership.

Teachers often come to the task of teaching reading without understanding the structure of language (Snow, Griffin, & Burns, 2006), the nature of language learning, or the methodologies that are supported by research (Foorman & Moats, 2004; Moats, 1994, 1999, 2004; Moats & Foorman, 2003, in press; Spear-Swerling & Brucker, 2004). Even after attending an excellent teacher preparation program, such as one that teaches the content required by the state of Colorado (see *Appendix B*), new teachers need more training. In addition, teachers usually have not had supervised practice implementing the instructional routines that are necessary for strong implementation. Teachers cannot learn all that they need to know in one workshop or one year. A longer-term model of capacity-building is much more realistic.

Lacking good research on the *stages of teacher development*, we must create models of teacher training based on the experience of researchers and educational leaders. We propose a growth model for teachers as follows:

Year 1

Summer Institute (5 days)

- Training in DIBELS or other screening (2 days), including instruction in what the assessments measure and why the measurement predicts more complex reading outcomes.

- Overview of foundational concepts in teaching reading, including video modeling of instruction and role-play of various lesson components.

- Preparation in the instructional routines of the core, comprehensive program in use in the school.

- Emphasis on being ready to carry out the first 6 weeks of instruction for that grade level.

Coaching and follow-up, by grade level

- Weekly grade-level meetings, with the focus alternating among: (a) analysis of student data; (b) preview of upcoming lessons and planning/modification of instructional plans; and (c) evaluation of student grouping decisions.

- In-class coaching, at least twice per month, using a student-centered coaching model (Hasbrouck & Denton, 2005).

- Three to five follow-up professional development days to review aspects of program implementation, including classroom management.

Year 2

Summer Institute (5 days)

- Study of English phonology and orthography (3 days).

- Application of concepts to analysis and modification of teaching materials and case studies to improve instruction at the word level.

- Continuation of in-class coaching and regular team meetings, with planned agendas.

- Three follow-up professional development days to focus on vocabulary and comprehension instruction and/or credit-bearing courses that treat topics in depth.

Year 3
Summer Institute (5 days)
• Seminars to examine additional topics in depth (e.g., teaching basic writing skills, working with ELL students in the classroom).
• Begin to select and prepare successful teachers to become coaches or team leaders; apprentice them with competent coaches.
Leadership Training
• Provide a two-day short course for principals and administrators on the characteristics of effective reading, language, and writing instruction at all tiers of student ability.
• Follow-up sessions to develop schoolwide plans for implementation.
Grade 3 and Up
• Three- to five-day institutes to teach basic word attack and spelling strategies, fluency-building approaches, guided text reading, structured written response, and study skills in the content areas.

Exercise 7.1 | Action Plan for Principals

• Before you leave this workshop, note your priorities for action.

Summary, Traits of Successful Schools	Indicators of Success	Priorities for Action
Strong leadership	• Conduct and lead data-analysis meetings. • Allocate budget for instructors and resources. • Adjust scheduling. • Assign staff. • Select research-based programs that fit student needs.	
Positive belief and teacher dedication	• Share data from successful schools. • Use incentives. • Motivate and reward effort.	

(continued)

Exercise 7.1 (continued)

Summary, Traits of Successful Schools	Indicators of Success	Priorities for Action
Data analysis	• Attend monthly grade-level data-analysis meetings. • Discuss and share ideas about student progress. • Support differentiated instruction. • Use data management systems.	
Effective scheduling	• Match staff to appropriate group assignments. • Prioritize responsibilities. • Protect common planning time. • Protect the reading block. • Schedule intervention sessions.	
Scientifically based programs	• Locate research-based core programs. • Select supplements according to student needs.	
Professional development	• Plan tiers, or levels, of PD. • Build in on-going supervision, follow-up, and coaching. • Create a contingency plan for new teachers. • Protect time for training, use incentives (e.g., credits, grants, partnerships).	
Parent involvement	• Provide babysitting services. • Provide food. • Schedule meetings at various times. • Consider the need for interpreters or second-language speakers. • Model how parents can help.	

Final Review, Module 1

1. List four ways in which spoken language, which is natural, differs from written language, which is not natural.

   _____

   _____

   _____

   _____

   _____

   _____

2. What is the implication of the fact that reading is not easy or natural for many students?

   _____

   _____

   _____

   _____

   _____

   _____

3. Why is scientifically conducted research an important source of guidance for our teaching practices?

   _____

   _____

   _____

   _____

   _____

4. The term "balanced literacy" is misleading. Explain why there is not an equal balance when we design instruction in all reading components. Cite research efforts that support your points.

   _____

   _____

   _____

   _____

   _____

(continued)

5. The following quote is from *Teaching Reading* Is *Rocket Science* (Moats, 1999, p. 16):

> "Those (skilled readers) who can most easily make sense of text are those who can most easily read nonsense."

Explain the reasoning behind this statement.

_____

_____

_____

_____

_____

_____

6. Below, draw the graphic organizer that represents Seidenberg and McClelland's (1989) four language–processing systems, and label all parts.

Appendix A

Instructor Script for *Exercise 2.2:*
Simulation of Learning to Read

1 (5 minutes)

Ask participants to cut out the symbol cards and sight words on pages 19 and 21 of their modules. You may choose to distribute a copy of these symbols and sight words from the Handouts Folder of the Presenter's Kit, LETRS Module 1, so that participants do not have to cut out pages in their modules. Alternatively, participants may use sticky notes to write their own symbols and words. If you choose this option, be sure that the symbols and words are correctly written on the notes before proceeding. Ten consonants and three vowels will be included in this exercise, as well as some sight words.

f	k	n	ŋ	θ	š	I

2

Select or make cards for irregular words.
- Ask participants to use their cut-out words (or sticky notes) of these four sight (or "heart") words. You will practice them later in the simulation.

ænd	**ə**	**ðə**	**wʌz**
and	a	the	was

3 (25 minutes, steps 3–17)

Lead teachers through the following steps at a comfortable pace. Start slowly, reviewing these three familiar symbols:

f	k	n

Present phoneme awareness and sound-symbol association.
Say:
- "First, we will review three sounds and symbols that you already know: **f, k, n**."

(continued)

- "Which symbol stands for /f/? Which one stands for /k/? Which one stands for /n/?"
- "When I point to a symbol, you say the sound: /f/, /k/, /n/."
- "I'll say a word, and you hold up the symbol and say the sound if you hear it in these words."
- "Say the sound /f/: Is there a /f/ in the word **phooey**?" (**yes**)
  "In **rough**?" (**yes**)
  "In **vendor**?" (**no**)
  "In **fender**?" (**yes**)
- "Say the sound /n/: Is there a /n/ in the word **sing**?" (**no**)
  "In **autumn**?" (**no**)
  "In **mnemonic**?" (**yes**)
- "Say the sound /k/: Is there a /k/ in the word **choir**?" (**yes**)
  "In **antique**?" (**yes**)
  "In **quilt**?" (**yes**)

4

- "Now we are going to learn four new sounds and symbols. Soon we will combine the sounds into words. The new symbols are:

| ŋ | θ | š | I |

- "First I'll say a sound. Then I'll say some words. If the sound is in the word I say, hold up your symbol card."

- "The sound is /ŋ/. / ŋ/ is the last sound in the word **wrong**. Say /ŋ/. What is your mouth doing? What is happening in your throat?" (The tongue is in the back of the throat; the sound goes through the nose; the sound is continuous; vocal cords are engaged.)

- "Now you say /ŋ/ and hold up your ŋ symbol card if you hear it in the word I say."

| **fang** (**yes**) | **lanky** (**yes**) | **single** (**yes**) | **angel** (**no**) |
| **English** (**yes**) | **angle** (**yes**) | **strange** (**no**) | |

Note: Some participants may put a /g/ after /ŋ/ because of dialect. Others may be confused by the spelling of words that use the letter **n** for /ŋ/. If you are asked, clarify that the sound /ŋ/ is spelled two ways (with **ng** and **n**), and that it is the third nasal sound in English. It is articulated right where the /g/ is also pronounced. Don't try to correct dialect difference.

Say:

- "The next symbol is **θ** (unvoiced /th/, as in **thin**). Say /th/. How am I making that sound?" (With my tongue between my teeth; by blowing air over the tongue; by turning off the voicebox.)
- "Now you say /th/ and hold up your **θ** symbol card if you hear it in the word I say."

thicket (yes)	**thread** (yes)	**both** (yes)	**filter** (no)
the (no)	**tangle** (no)	**theory** (yes)	**this** (no)

Note: Many participants will not have realized that there are *two* **th** sounds: a voiceless and a voiced. The voiced /th/ almost always occurs at the beginning of function words such as **the, this, then**, and **that**. Fortunately, both voiced and voiceless **th** sounds are spelled the same way in English.

Say:

- "The next new consonant symbol is **š** (/sh/). Describe how this sound is made." (Quiet, continuous, with the lips puckered and tongue forward.)
- "If you hear a /sh/ sound in a word I say, hold up your **š** card and say the sound."

mission (yes)	**chef** (yes)	**sugar** (yes)	**push** (yes)
vision (no)	**cheese** (no)	**cashier** (yes)	

- "The last consonant symbol in this set is **I** (/ĭ/), the first sound in **itch**. Say /ĭ/. What does your mouth do when you say /ĭ/?" (It's slightly open, somewhat smiley; the vocal cords are engaged; the air is not obstructed.)
- "Now you say /ĭ/ and hold up your **I** symbol card if you hear it in the word I say."

itchy (yes)	**innocent** (yes)	**crypt** (yes)	**nitrate** (no)
glimpse (yes)	**pen** (no)		

- "Now, we will practice. If I point to a symbol, you say the sound. If I say the sound, you point to the symbol." (Say the sounds in random order until each has been said two or three times.)

f	**k**	**n**	**I**	**θ**	**ŋ**	**š**

5

Blend these sounds into words.

- Point to each symbol, left to right, as you lead participants in blending the sounds; sweep your finger under the whole word as it is blended. (Do NOT use standard spelling as a cue to help out! Participants must learn the new symbol system.)

I n	θ I n	θ I ŋ	f I š
in	thin	thing	fish
f I n	š I n	θ I k	
fin	shin	thick	
k I n	k I ŋ	k I k	
kin	king	kick	

- Referring to the symbol words above, ask for a volunteer to:
  - Find the printed word that means the opposite of **thick**.
  - Find the printed word that means "ruler of a monarchy."
  - Point to his or her shin.
  - Demonstrate what a "kick" is.

6

- Read these words with consonant blends. Continue with the sound-blending technique.

k I ŋ k	I ŋ k	f I ŋ k	θ I ŋ k
kink	ink	fink	think

7

Practice recognizing irregular whole words.

Say:

- "In order to make sentences we have to learn some words by heart—by the way they look. Later we'll be learning the sounds in those words."
- Say a word and ask participants to hold up the correct card.

<u>**ænd**</u>	**ə**	**ð<u>ə</u>**	<u>**wʌz**</u>
and	a	the	was

Read phrases and sentences.

- Ask participants to read the following phrases and sentences out loud on their own, pointing with their fingers as they read. You may choose to have participants read round-robin style (i.e., one person reads a phrase/sentence, then the person sitting next to that person reads the next phrase/sentence, etc.) until all phrases and sentences are read. (You can prove that round-robin style is a poor practice method later in the debriefing section. Why is it a poor practice method? When reading this way, students pay attention only to *what they have to read*; they do not listen to others reading!)

θIk <u>ænd</u> θIn	(thick and thin)
<u>wʌz</u> ə fIŋk	(was a fink)
θIŋk In Iŋk	(think in ink)
kIk <u>ðə</u> šIn	(kick the shin)
kIŋk <u>ðə</u> θIŋ	(kink the thing)
fIšIŋ <u>wʌz</u> ə kIk.	(Fishing was a kick.)
<u>ðə</u> kIŋ <u>wʌz</u> fIšIŋ.	(The king was fishing.)
<u>ðə</u> kIŋ <u>wʌz</u> θIn.	(The king was thin.)
<u>ðə</u> fIš fIn <u>wʌz</u> θIn.	(The fish fin was thin.)
<u>wʌz</u> <u>ðə</u> θIŋ ə fIš?	(Was the thing a fish?)

Spell with letter tile cards.

Say:

- "Now I will say some words. Repeat them after me, select the sound cards you need, and put the letter tiles together to make the word."
- Dictate:
  - shick
  - thick
  - thing
  - ink
- "Write each word after you spell it with tiles."

Write dictated words, phrases, and sentences.

Say:

- "I am going to dictate some phrases and sentences to you. Please write these in your manual. We will check your work on the next slide."
- Dictate:
  - thick shin
  - thick and thin
  - think thin
  - The king was fishing.
  - The fish fin was thick.
  - Was the thing a fish?

Learn more sounds and symbols.

Say:

- "Now, we will learn three more sounds and symbols." (The pace picks up and there is less practice provided for each sound before word reading is attempted.)
- "Find or make the cards for these sounds and add them to your letter tiles."

w	t	ċ

- "Let's learn these new sounds:
  1. The first sound is /w/, as in **water** and **went**.
  2. The second sound is /t/, as in **table** and **team**.
  3. The third sound is /ċ/ (au), is in **paw** and **author**. It's a vowel."
- "Every syllable in English has a vowel. Say /ċ/ if you hear it in the word I say."

cra̲wl (yes)	**a̲udio** (yes)	**c̲ough** (yes)	**laugh** (no)	**potter** (no)
ca̲ution (yes)	**lo̲st** (yes)	**o̲ff** (yes—but it may depend on dialect!)		

Note: There may be dialect differences in the group. Some people believe there is no difference between the pronunciation of the vowel in **caught** and **cot**.

12

Say:

- "Listen. Write these symbols on a piece of paper." (Say all the sounds in random order.)

w	t	ċ	n	f
k	I	θ	ŋ	š

13

Read regular words.

- Encourage participants to read these words, pointing to each one as you lead them through the list. (You might choose to call on individual participants to decode words in front of others to illustrate how stressful this can be for students.)

ċn	ċf	tċŋ	tċk
θċt	tċt	fċt	kċt
θċŋ	kċŋ	kċf	wċnt
wIš	wIŋ	wIn	wIθ
wIkIŋ		wċkIŋ	

14

Review sight words.

Say:

- "Let's review sight words and then add some new ones. Why are they called *heart* words?" (They must be memorized so that you know them "by heart.")
- "Here are a few new sight words."

<u>aı̣</u>	<u>tu</u>	<u>ju</u>
I	to	you

- Hold up these symbols and simply tell participants what these words are. Keep your brisk pace.

(continued)

Say:

* "Hold up the card for the word I say. Then mix up your cards and read the words."

<u>tu</u> to	ðə the	<u>ju</u> you	<u>wʌz</u> was
ænd and	ə a	<u>aɪ</u> I	

Read these phrases and sentences.

* Encourage participants to read these phrases and sentences aloud, on their own. (You may choose to ask individuals to read these in front of the group.)

a. θɪŋk, tċk, <u>ænd</u> wċk
(think, talk, and walk)

b. wċnt <u>ænd</u> wɪš
(want and wish)

c. θɪŋk ðə θċt
(think the thought)

d. tċkɪŋ ċn <u>ænd</u> ċf
(talking on and off)

e. ðə kɪŋ kċt ə kċf.
(The king caught a cough.)

f. kɪŋ kċŋ fċt ċf ðə θɪŋ.
(King Kong fought off the thing.)

g. <u>aɪ</u> wċnt <u>tu</u> fɪš wɪθ <u>ju</u>.
(I want to fish with you.)

h. <u>ju</u> wċkt, θɪŋkɪŋ θċts ċn <u>ænd</u> ċf.
(You walked, thinking thoughts on and off.)

16

Teach a new sound-symbol correspondence.
- Briefly teach this new sound-symbol correspondence. Hold up the card and show it on the PowerPoint slide:

> Λ = a vowel, the first sound in the word **up**

Say:
- "Do you hear Λ in these words?"

l<u>o</u>ve (yes)	cot (no)	d<u>o</u>ne (yes)

- Present the new sight word and its definition:

> <u>Λv</u>
> of

17

- Ask participants to chorally read the following story aloud.

> <u>ðə</u> kɪŋ <u>wʌz</u> θɪŋkɪŋ <u>ʌv</u> fʌn æn<u>d</u>
> wċntɪd <u>tu</u> fɪš. "aj wċnt ə θɪk fɪš,"
> θċt <u>ðə</u> kɪŋ. <u>ðə</u> kɪŋ kċt ə θɪn fɪš.
> "aj wɪš <u>ðə</u> fɪš <u>wʌz</u> θɪk," wɪšṛ <u>ðə</u>
> kɪŋ. <u>ðə</u> kɪŋ šċkt <u>ðə</u> fɪš æn<u>d</u> kʌt
> <u>ðə</u> kɪŋk ɪn <u>ðə</u> θɪŋ. <u>ðə</u> fɪš wɪŋkt
> <u>tu</u> <u>ðə</u> kɪŋ!

Translation: The king was thinking of fun and wanted to fish. "I want a thick fish," thought the king. The king caught a thin fish. "I wish the fish was thick," wished the king. The king shocked the fish and cut the kink in the thing. The fish winked to the king!

Appendix B

Colorado Teacher Preparation Program Criteria for Literacy Courses

Checklist for Literacy Courses*

Assessment

Teacher Candidates will:

a. Understand the **basic concepts involved in test selection administration, standardized administration techniques, and interpretation** (reliability, validity, and standard error, norm-referenced, and criterion-referenced).

b. Comprehend the meaning of **basic statistics** such as normal curve equivalents, percentile ranks, stanines, quartiles, standard scores, and grade equivalents for interpretation of data.

c. Understand the **purposes of different kinds of assessments** (screening, progress monitoring, diagnostic, and outcome).

d. **Understand the legal and ethical issues** in the fair and meaningful evaluation of students in the classroom, including confidentiality, informed consent, privacy, and bias.

e. Identify independent, **objective sources for reviews** of valid and reliable assessment tools.

f. Select, administer, and interpret reliable and valid classroom **screening** measures to identify students at risk for reading difficulty.

g. **Select reading texts** appropriate for the identified instructional outcomes (e.g., decodable text for building word-reading accuracy and fluency or literature for vocabulary and comprehension).

h. Select, administer, and interpret **progress-monitoring** assessments to evaluate students' progress toward an instructional goal, to determine effectiveness of instruction / intervention, and to regularly articulate progress to students.

i. Analyze and incorporate the **results of end-of-year achievement tests** into a body of evidence for the development of instructional plans (e.g., ILPs).

j. **Translate technical concepts** and terminology of assessments into concrete, clear, and culturally sensitive language for reporting to colleagues, students, and parents.

* Adapted by the state of Colorado in 2006 from Maryland DOE Reading Course Revision Guidelines and Connecticut DOE Blueprint for Reading Achievmeent.

Phonology and Phoneme Awareness

Teacher Candidates will:

a. Identify and **pronounce the speech sounds** of English.

b. Know a research-based scope and sequence for **phonemic and phonological awareness** instruction based on the developmental progression of skills: rhyme, syllables, onset-rime, phoneme differentiation.

c. Apply systematic, explicit techniques for teaching **phonological awareness**: speech sound identification, matching, blending, and segmenting.

d. Know the **predictive value of phonemic awareness** in early reading development.

e. Select, use, and interpret **assessments of phonological and phonemic awareness** and use them to screen for reading difficulties, to monitor student progress, and to make instructional decisions.

Phonics and the Alphabetic Principle

Teacher Candidates will:

a. Recognize the development of **print concepts in young children**: print conveys meaning, printed words are composed of letters, print is read from left to right and top to bottom, and spoken words match printed words.

b. Know the **predictive value of letter-naming fluency** in early reading development.

c. Know a research-based scope and sequence, progressing from easy to more difficult, for **teaching the alphabetic principle, phonics (phoneme-grapheme associations), and orthographic patterns**.

d. Use a systematic, explicit approach to **teach phonics and word analysis in decoding**.

e. Apply techniques for teaching automatic **recognition of common phonetically irregular (exception) words in English**.

f. Understand the role of the various **syllable structures** (open, closed, silent-**e**, vowel team, consonant-**le**, **r**-controlled) and **morphemes** (prefixes, roots, suffixes) in fluent recognition of multisyllable words.

g. Understand the importance of the use of **decodable and controlled text** to reinforce word decoding recognition skills that have been taught.

h. Select, use, and interpret **phonics surveys, writing samples, and word identification assessments** to measure alphabetic knowledge and word decoding skills and use them to screen for reading difficulties, to monitor student progress, and to make instructional decisions.

i. Use a systematic, explicit approach to teach orthographic and morphological **patterns in spelling**.

j. Understand the **reciprocal relationship** between learning orthographic patterns for reading (**decoding**) and spelling (**encoding**).

k. Select, use, and interpret **diagnostic spelling inventories** (e.g., differences between phonetic and lexical spelling patterns) and use them to screen for spelling difficulties, to monitor student progress, and to make instructional decisions.

Reading Comprehension

Teacher Candidates will:

a. Understand the relationships among **listening comprehension, language comprehension, and reading comprehension** and how they change as reading skill develops.

b. Understand the **knowledge and processes used in reading comprehension**: decoding, word-naming speed, inference-making, comprehension monitoring, grammatical awareness, background and prior knowledge, word-meaning knowledge.

c. Know the **factors that influence reading comprehension**—the reader, the text, the reading task, the environmental context, and the interactions among them.

d. **Explicitly teach** the conventions and **text structures** associated with a variety of genre, including literary texts (poems, plays, narrative stories, novels) and expository texts (textbooks, electronic texts, essays, technical reports).

e. **Explicitly teach** the differences between, and the **strategies for, analysis of components of literary texts** (e.g., theme, narrator's point of view) **and expository texts** (e.g., author's purpose, position, or stance on a subject).

f. **Explicitly teach** research-based text **comprehension strategies** (e.g., metacognitive monitoring strategies, graphic and semantic organizers, answering questions, generating questions, story structure, summarizing) to be used before, during, and after reading.

g. Scaffold discussions by asking questions that increase engagement in **literary response and analysis**, expand student thinking, and support the affective dimensions of reading comprehension.

h. Select, use, and interpret formal and informal **assessments of student reading comprehension** and use them to screen for reading difficulties, to monitor student progress, and to make instructional decisions.

i. Use assessment data to plan **interventions to foster reading comprehension** using research-based programs and practices.

j. Know the interrelationship of **reading comprehension, fluent decoding skills, background knowledge**, and vocabulary knowledge.

Reading Fluency

Teacher Candidates will:

a. Identify **expectations / norms for fluency** as reading skill develops.

b. **Identify factors that may impact fluency** (e.g. word reading skill, vocabulary knowledge, text difficulty, background knowledge, reason for reading, type of text).

c. Identify and apply explicit and implicit **oral passage reading techniques** for increasing reading fluency (e.g., increasing time spent reading at independent level, alternate oral reading, timed repeated readings, simultaneous oral reading, and timed speed drills).

d. **Select, use, and interpret assessments of reading fluency** and use them to screen for reading difficulties, to monitor student progress, and to make instructional decisions targeted for improved student outcomes.

Content-Area Reading

Teacher Candidates will:

a. Know the importance of **supported reading practice** in increasing reading fluency and comprehension.

b. Select and apply text **comprehension strategies for literacy in content areas**.

c. Know strategies to develop **parent-school and school-community** support to promote **independent reading practice**.

d. Collaborate with school-based teams to identify, evaluate, and select classroom **materials** that **support content-area reading**.

e. Select appropriate **independent reading materials** to match student reading performance.

Oral Language Development

Teacher Candidates will:

a. Understand how oral language develops and the relationship among oral **language proficiency and reading, spelling, and writing proficiency**.

b. **Know the organization of language**: phonology, orthography, morphology, syntax, semantic networks, and discourse structure.

c. Discern the differences between **informal/conversational language and formal/literate/academic language** that can be problematic in reading and writing.

d. Understand the **historical evolution of the English language** and the alphabetic writing system.

e. Understand the impact of background knowledge, **language differences, difficulties, and disorders** on literacy acquisition.

Vocabulary

Teacher Candidates will:

a. Know the scientific research on how oral and written **vocabulary develops** in first- and second-language learners.

b. Understand the **role of morphology in written English**, including Anglo-Saxon, Latin, and Greek-derived morphemes.

c. **Understand and apply** morphological and etymological similarities and differences in languages in teaching **first- and second-language learners**.

d. Recognize the aspects of **learning word meanings**, including multiple meanings and uses of words, idiomatic expressions, the limitations of dictionary definitions, the demands of categorical and hierarchical reasoning, or insufficient examples of contextual use.

e. Identify research-supported **approaches to selecting words** for in-depth vocabulary instruction.

f. **Identify and use direct and indirect techniques** for vocabulary instruction in the classroom.

Writing

Teacher Candidates will:

a. Understand the reciprocity between **foundational writing skills** (handwriting, spelling, knowledge of conventions, fluent transcription, verbal ideation, grammar) and **higher order thinking skills** in developing **high-quality written composition**.

b. Understand the **writing process**—planning, composing, revising, and editing of written products.

c. Explicitly teach and encourage the use of **formal language patterns** (correct grammar and forms) and academic vocabulary in student writing.

d. **Analyze students' writing samples** for phonological, orthographic, syntactic, and semantic patterns of use, and plan instruction based on findings.

e. Teach **basic mechanics** of writing (capitalization, punctuation, handwriting).

f. Teach **sentence structure** (avoiding sentence fragments, using varied sentence lengths).

g. Teach **organization and paragraphing**.

h. Develop students' **clarity, descriptiveness, and elaboration** when writing.

State Standards and Assessments

Teacher Candidates will:

a. **Know the** Colorado Model Content **Standards and Benchmarks** for Reading and Writing.

b. Know the **Colorado Basic Literacy Act (CBLA) Reading Proficiencies** for Kindergarten, 1st, 2nd, and 3rd grades.

c. Assess CBLA proficiencies and use assessment data to develop an Individual Literacy Plan (ILP).

d. Use **CSAP assessment frameworks** in reading and writing, including assessment objectives for each grade level to develop curriculum that will support reading and writing achievement.

e. Know the progression of underlying skills (phonemic awareness, phonics, vocabulary, language comprehension, spelling, and writing skills) necessary to demonstrate proficiency on the reading and writing CSAP tests.

f. Identify and analyze **examples of** unsatisfactory, partially proficient, proficient, and advanced **student work** at various grade levels and the implication for instruction.

g. **When students are not proficient on CSAP**, select, use, and interpret **assessments of underlying reading skills** and use data to develop a plan for intervention.

Appendix C

Extension Activities

Identify the Essential Components of Reading Instruction

- Below are examples of instructional routines and activities from various literacy programs. Identify which of the six major components of reading instruction is addressed by each activity:
  1. phonological awareness and letter knowledge
  2. phonics, spelling, and word study
  3. reading fluency
  4. vocabulary development
  5. reading comprehension
  6. written composition

_____ A teacher asks students to summarize the main idea of a passage.

_____ Students list as many meanings as they can think of for the word **shock**.

_____ Using timers, student partners time each other to see how many words each can read accurately in one minute while reading a familiar passage aloud.

_____ A teacher says /f/ /l/ /ē/ and asks students to blend the sounds.

_____ A teacher points to the written word **matador** and asks students how many syllables are in that word.

_____ Students move three chips or markers into boxes as they say the single sounds of the word **house**—/h/ /ou/ /s/.

_____ Before reading, students browse their storybooks to predict the main content of the story and to ask questions about what they will learn.

_____ A teacher tells students that –**dge** and –**ge** both stand for /j/ at the ends of words. Students then sort a group of 20 –**ge** and –**dge** words to determine when the –**dge** spelling is used.

_____ Students reread words with known phonic patterns so that they can recognize them instantly without having to sound them out laboriously.

_____ Students are directed to read this sentence and guess at the meaning of the word **burden**: The pilgrim's _burden_ weighed heavily on his shoulders as he ascended the steep mountain trail.

Survey the Components in Your Core Program

(This exercise is used with permission of Mary Dahlgren and is excerpted from her presentation "Bridging Activities: Linking LETRS to the Core, Comprehensive Reading Program")

Materials needed

- Teacher Edition (TE) of a core, comprehensive reading program (one TE per group)
- Five colors of small self-stick notes with the following labels, each written on a different color note: *PA, Phonics, Vocab, Fluency, Comp.*

- Participants work in grade-level groups, reviewing a weekly lesson outline and determining which reading instruction components are addressed daily and throughout the week with the colored notes. (A well-designed program in the primary grades will address all five reading instruction components, with extra emphasis on the decoding subskills of letter-naming, phonology, and phonics.)

- After the groups have placed their labeled notes in the TEs, discuss the changes in emphasis that are apparent over grade levels:
    1. Where do you begin to see changing occurring?
    2. How does this information help to plan instruction?
    3. If a third-grade program has little or no evidence of phonological instruction, what does this mean for students who have still not developed in that area?

- Leave all of the TEs open on the tables and take a few minutes to rotate around the room to see the changes in the core reading program instruction in relation to the components of instruction.

Glossary

Advanced concepts are indicated with an asterisk (*).

*AAVE: African American vernacular English, also called Ebonics or Black English; a dialect with phonological, semantic, and syntactic features that originated with African languages brought to the Americas by slaves

affix: a morpheme or a meaningful part of a word that is attached before or after a root to modify its meaning; a category that includes prefixes, suffixes, and infixes

*affricate: a speech sound with features of both a fricative and a stop; in English, /ch/ and /j/ are affricates

*affrication: the pronunciation of /t/ as /ch/ in words such as **nature**, and /d/ as /j/ in words such as **educate**

alphabetic principle: the principle that letters are used to represent individual phonemes in the spoken word; a critical insight for beginning reading and spelling

alphabetic writing system: a system of symbols that represent each consonant and vowel sound in a language

Anglo-Saxon: Old English, a Germanic language spoken in Britain before the invasion of the Norman French in 1066

base word: a free morpheme, usually of Anglo-Saxon origin, to which affixes can be added

*bound morpheme: a meaningful part of a word that makes words only in combination with other morphemes; includes inflections, roots, prefixes, and derivational suffixes

chunk: a group of letters, processed as a unit, that corresponds to a piece of a word, usually a consonant cluster, rime pattern, syllable, or morpheme

closed sound: a consonant sound made by using the tongue, teeth, or lips to obstruct the air as it is pushed through the vocal cavity

cognate: a word in one language that shares a common ancestor and common meanings with a word in another language

closed syllable: a written syllable containing a single vowel letter that ends in one or more consonants; the vowel sound is short

cluster: adjacent consonants that appear before or after a vowel; a consonant blend

★**coarticulation**: speaking phonemes together so that the feature of each spreads to neighboring phonemes and all the segments are joined into one linguistic unit (a syllable)

concept: an idea that links other facts, words, and ideas together into a coherent whole

consensus: agreement in the scientific community on specific truths that have emanated from a series of studies about a specific problem or issue

consonant: a phoneme (speech sound) that is not a vowel and that is formed by obstructing the flow of air with the teeth, lips, or tongue; also called a *closed sound* in some instructional programs; English has 25 consonant phonemes

consonant cluster: (see *cluster*)

consonant digraph: a two-letter combination that represents one speech sound that is not represented by either letter alone

consonant-le syllable: a written syllable found at the ends of words such as **dawdle**, **single**, and **rubble**

context: the language that surrounds a given word or phrase (linguistic context), or the field of meaningful associations that surrounds a given word or phrase (experiential context)

context processor: the neural networks that bring background knowledge and discourse to bear as word meanings are processed

correlational studies: studies that show the strength of relationship between two or more variables, but that ordinarily are not sufficient to prove a causal relationship between or among those variables

cross-sectional: a type of study that draws samples of students from different age groups or grade-level groups

cumulative instruction: teaching that proceeds in additive steps, building on what was previously taught

decodable text: text in which a high proportion (i.e., 70–90 percent) of words comprise sound-symbol relationships that have already been taught; used to provide practice with specific decoding skills; a bridge between learning phonics and the application of phonics in independent reading of text

decoding: the ability to translate a word from print to speech, usually by employing knowledge of sound-symbol correspondences; also the act of deciphering a new word by sounding it out

★**deep alphabetic orthography**: a writing system that represents both phonemes and morphemes

★**derivational suffix**: a type of bound morpheme; a suffix—such as **-ity**, **-ive**, and **-ly**—that can change the part of speech of the root or base word to which it is added

dialects: mutually intelligible versions of the same language with systematic differences in phonology, word use, and/or grammatical rules

digraph: a two-letter combination (e.g., **th, ph**) that stands for a single phoneme in which neither letter represents its usual sound

diphthong: a vowel produced by the tongue shifting position during articulation; a vowel that has a glide; a vowel that feels as if it has two parts, especially the vowels spelled **ou** and **oi**; some linguistics texts also classify all tense (long) vowels as diphthongs

direct instruction: instruction in which the teacher defines and teaches a concept, guides students through its application, and arranges extended guided practice for students until mastery is achieved

discourse structure: organizational conventions in longer segments of oral or written language

double deficit: an impairment of both phonological processing and speed of word recognition

dyslexia: an impairment of reading accuracy and fluency attributable to an underlying phonological deficit

effect size: a statistic that measures the impact of an intervention on student performance in terms of standard deviation units

★**encoding**: producing written symbols for spoken language; also, spelling by sounding out

★**flap**: the tongue rising behind the teeth to produce a diminished /t/ or /d/ in the middle of words such as **water, better, little**, and **rudder**

★**fricative**: a consonant sound created by forcing air through a narrow opening in the vocal tract; includes /f/, /v/, /s/, /z/, /sh/, /zh/, and /th/

fluency: in reading, to read with sufficient speed to support understanding

generalization: a pattern in the spelling system that applies to a substantial family of words

★**glide**: a type of speech sound that glides immediately into a vowel; includes /h/, /w/, and /y/

grapheme: a letter or letter combination that spells a phoneme; can be one, two, three, or four letters in English (e.g., **e, ei, igh, eigh**)

inflection: a type of bound morpheme; a grammatical ending that does not change the part of speech of a word but that marks its tense, number, or degree in English (e.g., **–s, –ed, –ing**)

integrated: lesson components that are interwoven and flow smoothly together

★**lexicon**: the name for the mental dictionary in every person's linguistic processing system

★liquid: the speech sounds /l/ and /r/ that have vowel-like qualities and no easily definable point of articulation

logographic: a form of writing that represents the meaning of words and concepts with pictures or signs; contrasts with writing systems that represent speech sounds

longitudinal: a type of study that selects and then follows subjects over a long period of time

long-term memory: the memory system that stores information beyond 24 hours

★marker: in linguistics, a letter that has no sound of its own but that indicates the sound of another letter or letter combination, such as the letter **u** in the word **guard** that makes the /g/ a hard sound

meaning processor: the neural networks that attach meanings to words that have been heard or decoded

meta-analysis: a statistical analysis of the combined results of a series of studies that all address the same issue or problem

★metalinguistic awareness: an acquired level of awareness of language structure and function that allows us to reflect on and consciously manipulate the language we use

Middle English: the form of English spoken between the years 1200–1600, after the French Norman invasion of England and before the time of Shakespeare

★monosyllabic: having only one syllable

morpheme: the smallest meaningful unit of a language; it may be a word or part of a word; it may be one or more syllables (e.g., **un-inter-rupt-ible**)

morphology: the study of the meaningful units in a language and how they are combined in word formation

morphophonemic: having to do with both sound and meaning

multisyllabic: having more than one syllable

narrative: the type of text that tells about sequences of events, usually with the structure of a fiction or nonfiction story; often contrasted with expository text, which reports factual information and the relationships among ideas

NRP: Initialism for the Report of the National Reading Panel (National Institute of Child Health and Human Development, 2000)

onset-rime: the natural division of a syllable into two parts, the onset coming before the vowel and the rime including the vowel and what follows it (e.g., **pl-an, shr-ill**)

orthographic processor: the neural networks responsible for perceiving, storing, and retrieving letter sequences in words

orthography: a writing system for representing language

phoneme: a speech sound that combines with others in a language system to make words; English has 40 to 44 phonemes, according to various linguists

phoneme awareness (also, **phonemic awareness**): the conscious awareness that words are made up of segments of our own speech that are represented with letters in an alphabetic orthography

phonics: the study of the relationships between letters and the sounds they represent; also used as a descriptor for code-based instruction in reading (i.e., "the phonics approach" or "phonic reading")

phonological awareness: metalinguistic awareness of all levels of the speech sound system, including word boundaries, stress patterns, syllables, onset–rime units, and phonemes; a more encompassing term than *phoneme awareness*

phonological processor: a neural network in the frontal and temporal areas of the brain, usually the left cerebral hemisphere, that is specialized for speech-sound perception, memory, retrieval, and pronunciation

phonological working memory: the "online" memory system that remembers speech long enough to extract meaning from it, or that holds onto words during writing; a function of the phonological processor

phonology: the rule system within a language by which phonemes can be sequenced, combined, and pronounced to make words

★**pragmatics**: the system of rules and conventions for using language and related gestures in a social context

prefix: a morpheme that precedes a root and that contributes to or modifies the meaning of a word; a common linguistic unit in Latin-based words

qualitative research: research that relies on descriptive methodologies, including observational, case study, and ethnographic research; useful for hypothesis-generation

quantitative research: research that relies on measurement and statistical control of variables; preferable for determining cause and effect

randomized experiments: in research, experiments in which subjects are randomly assigned to the conditions that are being studied and compared

reading fluency: the speed of reading; the ability to read text with sufficient speed to support comprehension

root: a bound morpheme, usually of Latin origin, that cannot stand alone but that is used to form a family of words with related meanings

schwa: the "empty" vowel in an unaccented syllable, such as the last syllables of **circ<u>u</u>s** and **bag<u>e</u>l**

semantics: the study of word and phrase meanings and relationships

★**shallow alphabetic orthography**: a writing system that represents speech sounds with letters directly and consistently, using one letter for each sound

silent letter spelling: a spelling structure that consists of a consonant grapheme with a silent letter and a letter that corresponds to the vocalized sound (e.g., **kn**, **wr**, **gn**)

sound–symbol correspondence: same as *phoneme-grapheme correspondence*; the rules and patterns by which letters and letter combinations represent speech sounds

stop: a type of consonant that is spoken with one push of breath and not continued or carried out, including /p/, /b/, /t/, /d/, /k/, and /g/

structural analysis: the study of affixes, base words, and roots

suffix: a derivational morpheme (added to a root or base word) that often changes the word's part of speech and modifies its meaning

★**syllabic consonants**: /m/, /n/, /l/, and /r/ can do the job of a vowel and make an unaccented syllable at the ends of words such as **rhythm**, **mitten**, **little**, and **letter**

syllable: the unit of pronunciation that is organized around a vowel; it may or may not have consonants before or after the vowel

syntax: the system of rules governing permissible word order in sentences

vowel: one of a set of 15 vowel phonemes in English, not including vowel-**r** combinations; an open phoneme that is the nucleus of every syllable; classified by tongue position and height (e.g., high to low, front to back)

whole language: a philosophy of reading instruction that de-emphasizes the importance of phonics and phonology and that emphasizes the importance of learning to recognize words as wholes through encounters in meaningful contexts

word recognition: the instant recognition of a whole word in print

Bibliography

Adams, M. (1990). *Beginning to read: Thinking and learning about print*. Cambridge, MA: MIT Press.

Adams, M. (1998). The three-cueing system. In J. Osborn & F. Lehr (Eds.), *Literacy for all: Issues in teaching and learning*. New York: Guilford Press.

Anderson, R. C., Heibert, E. H., Scott, J. A., & Wilkinson, I. A. G. (1985). *Becoming a nation of readers*. Champaign, IL: University of Illinois, Center for the Study of Reading.

Anderson, R. C., Wilson, P. T., & Fielding, L. G. (1988). Growth in reading and how children spend their time outside of school. *Reading Research Quarterly, 23*, 285–303.

Arguelles, M., & Baker, S. (in press). *Teaching English language learners: A supplementary* LETRS® *module*. Longmont, CO: Sopris West Educational Services.

Berninger, V., & Richards, T. (2002). *Brain literacy for educators and psychologists*. Amsterdam: Academic Press.

Birsh, J. (Ed.) (2005). *Multisensory teaching of basic language skills*. Baltimore: Paul H. Brookes.

Blachman, B. A., Schatschneider, C., Fletcher, J. M., Francis, D. J., Clonan, S., Shaywitz, B., et al. (2004). Effects of intensive reading remediation for second and third graders. *Journal of Educational Psychology, 96*, 444–461.

Carroll, L. (1993; originally published 1941). *Through the looking glass and what Alice found there*. New York: HarperCollins.

Catone, W. V., & Brady, S. (2005). The inadequacy of individual educational program goals for high school students with word-level reading difficulties. *Annals of Dyslexia, 55*(1), 53–78.

Chall, J. (1996). *Stages of reading development* (2nd ed.). Orlando, FL: Harcourt Brace.

Chenoweth, K. (2007). *It's being done: Academic success in unexpected schools*. Cambridge, MA: Harvard University Press.

Comrie, B., Matthews, S., & Polinsky, M. (Eds.). (1996). *The atlas of languages: The origin and development of languages throughout the world*. London: Quarto Publishing.

Connor, C. D., Morrison, F. J., & Underwood, P. S. (2007). A second chance in second grade: The independent and cumulative impact of first- and second-grade reading instruction and students' letter-word reading skill growth. *Scientific Studies of Reading, 11*(3), 199–233.

Crawford, E. C., & Torgesen, J. K. (July 2006). *Teaching all children to read: Practices from Reading First schools with strong intervention outcomes*. Presented at the Florida Principal's Leadership Conference. Retrievable from http://www.fcrr.org/science/sciencePresentationscrawford.htm

Cunningham, A., & Stanovich, K. (1998). What reading does for the mind. *American Educator, 22*(1 & 2), 8–15.

Curtis, S. (1977). *Genie: A linguistic study of a modern-day "wild child."* New York: Academic Press.

Denton, C., Foorman, B., & Mathes, P. (2003). Schools that "Beat the Odds": Implications for reading instruction. *Remedial and Special Education, 24,* 258–261.

Denton, C., Vaughn, S., & Fletcher, J. (2003). Bringing research-based practice in reading intervention to scale. *Learning Disabilities Research and Practice, 18,* 201–211.

Eden, G., & Moats, L. (2002). The role of neuroscience in the remediation of students with dyslexia. *Nature Neuroscience, 5,* 1080–1084.

EdSource. (2003). *California's lowest performing schools: Who they are, the challenges they face, and how they're improving.* Palo Alto, CA: Author.

Ehri, L. (1996). Development of the ability to read words. In R. Barr, M. Kamil, P. B. Mosenthal, & P. D. Pearson (Eds.), *Handbook of reading research: Volume II* (pp. 383–418). Mahwah, NJ: Lawrence Erlbaum.

Ehri, L. C. (1997). Sight word learning in normal readers and dyslexics. In B. Blachman (Ed.), *Foundations of reading acquisition and dyslexia* (pp. 163–189). Mahwah, NJ: Lawrence Erlbaum.

Ehri, L. C. (1998). Grapheme-phoneme knowledge is essential for learning to read words in English. In J. L. Matsala & L. C. Ehri (Eds.), *Word recognition in beginning literacy* (pp. 3–40). Mahwah, NJ: Lawrence Erlbaum.

Ehri, L. C. (2004). Teaching phonemic awareness and phonics: An explanation of the national reading panel meta-analysis. In P. McCardle & V. Chhabra (Eds.), *The voice of evidence in reading research* (pp. 153–186). Baltimore: Paul H. Brookes.

Ehri, L., & Snowling, M. (2004). Developmental variation in word recognition. In A. C. Stone, E. R. Silliman, B. J. Ehren, & K. Apel (Eds.), *Handbook of language and literacy: Development and disorders* (pp. 443–460). New York: Guilford Press.

Elmore, R. (2004). *School reform from the inside out: Policy, practice, and performance.* Cambridge, MA: Harvard University Press.

Fletcher, J., Denton, C., Fuchs, L., & Vaughn, S. (2005). Multi-tiered reading instruction: Linking general education and special education. In S. Richardson & J. Gilger (Eds.), *Research-based education and intervention: What we need to know* (pp. 21–43). Baltimore: International Dyslexia Association.

Fletcher, J., & Francis, D. J. (2004). Scientifically based educational research: Questions, designs, and methods. In P. McCardle & V. Chhabra (Eds.), *The voice of evidence in reading research* (pp. 59–80). Baltimore: Paul H. Brookes.

Fletcher, J., Lyon, G. R., Fuchs, L., & Barnes, M. A. (2007). *Learning disabilities: From identification to intervention.* New York: Guilford Press.

Foorman, B. F. (Ed.). (2003). *Preventing and remediating reading difficulties: Bringing science to scale.* Baltimore: York Press.

Foorman, B. R., Francis, D. J., Fletcher, J. M., Schatschneider, C., & Mehta, P. (1998). The role of instruction in learning to read: Preventing reading failure in at-risk-children. *Journal of Educational Psychology, 90,* 37–55.

Foorman, B. R., Francis, D. J., Shaywitz, S. E., Shaywitz, B. A., & Fletcher, J. M. (1997). The case for early reading intervention. In B. Blachman (Ed.), *Foundations of reading acquisition and dyslexia: Implications for early intervention* (pp. 243–264). Baltimore: Paul H. Brookes.

Foorman, B. R., & Moats, L. C. (2004). Conditions for sustaining research-based practices in early reading instruction. *Remedial and Special Education, 25*(1), 51–60.

Fuchs, D., & Fuchs, L. S. (2006). Introduction to response to intervention: What, why, and how valid is it? *Reading Research Quarterly, 41*, 93–99.

Glaser, D. (2005). *ParaReading: A training guide for tutors.* Longmont, CO: Sopris West Educational Services.

Glaser, D., & Moats, L. C. (2008). *LETRS® Foundations: An introduction to language and literacy.* Longmont, CO: Sopris West Educational Services.

Good, R. H., & Kaminski, R. (2010). *DIBELS Next: Dynamic indicators of basic early literacy skills,* (7th ed.). Longmont, CO: Cambium/Sopris.

Good, R. H., & Kaminski, R. (2005). *Dynamic indicators of basic early reading skills* (DIBELS®) (6th ed.). Longmont, CO: Sopris West Educational Services.

Good, R. H., Simmons, D. C., & Kame'enui, E. J. (2001). The importance and decision-making utility of a continuum of fluency-based indicators of foundational reading skills for third-grade high-stakes outcomes. *Scientific Studies of Reading, 5*, 257–288.

Gough, P., & Tunmer, W. (1986). Decoding, reading and reading disability. *Remedial and Special Education, 7*, 6–10.

Hamilton, C., & Shinn, M. (2003). Characteristics of word callers: An investigation of the accuracy of teachers' judgments of reading comprehension and oral reading skills. *School Psychology Review, 32*(2), 228–240.

Hart Paulson, L. (in press). *Early childhood LETRS®.* Longmont, CO: Sopris West Educational Services.

Hasbrouck, J., & Denton, C. (2005). *The reading coach: A how-to manual for success.* Longmont, CO: Sopris West Educational Services.

Hodgson, B. (1995). *World of baby animals.* Lancaster, England: Gazelle Books.

Hudson, R. R., High, L., & Al Otaiba, S. (2007). Dyslexia and the brain: What does current research tell us? *The Reading Teacher, 60*(6), 506–515.

Jetton, T., & Dole, J. (Eds.). (2004). *Adolescent literacy research and practice.* New York: Guilford Press.

Jimerson, S. R. (2001). Meta-analysis of grade retention research: Implications for practice in the 21st century. *School Psychology Review, 30*(3), 420–437.

Kame'enui, E. J., Carnine, D. W., Dixon, R. C., Simmons, D. C., & Coyne, M. D. (2002). *Effective teaching strategies that accommodate diverse learners.* Upper Saddle River, NJ: Merrill Prentice Hall.

Katzir, T., Kim, Y., Wolf, M., O'Brien, B., Kennedy, B., Lovett, M., et al. (2006). Reading fluency: The whole is more than the parts. *Annals of Dyslexia, 56*(1), 51–82.

Keogh, B. (2004). The importance of longitudinal research for early intervention practices. In P. McCardle & V. Chhabra (Eds.), *The voice of evidence in reading research* (pp. 81–102). Baltimore: Paul H. Brookes.

King, R., & Torgesen, J. (2006). Improving the effectiveness of reading instruction in one elementary school: A description of the process. In P. Blaunstein & R. Lyon (Eds.), *It doesn't have to be this way.* Lanham, MD: Scarecrow Press.

Kuhl, P., Williams, K., Lacerda, F., Stevens, K., & Lindblom, B. (1992). Linguistic experience alters phonetic perception in infants by 6 months of age. *Science, 255,* 606–608.

Leach, J. M., Scarborough, H. S., & Rescorla, L. (2003). Late-emerging reading disabilities. *Journal of Educational Psychology, 95*(2), 211–224.

Learning First Alliance. (2000). *Every child reading: A professional development guide.* Washington, DC: Learning First Alliance.

Liberman, I. Y., Shankweiler, D., & Liberman, A. M. (1989). The alphabetic principle and learning to read. In D. Shankweiler & I. Liberman (Eds.), *Phonology and reading disability: Solving the reading puzzle* (pp. 1–33). Ann Arbor: University of Michigan Press.

Lyon, G. R., & Chhabra, V. (2004). The science of reading research. *Educational Leadership, 61,* 12–17.

Lyon, G. R., & Moats, L.C. (1997). Critical conceptual and methodological considerations in reading intervention research. *Journal of Learning Disabilities, 30*(6), 578–588.

Lyon, R., Shaywitz, S., & Shaywitz, D. (2003). *A definition of dyslexia. Annals of Dyslexia, 53,* 1–14.

Mathes, P. G., Denton, C.A., Fletcher, J. M., Anthony, J. L., Francis, D. J., & Schatschneider, C. (2005). The effects of theoretically different instruction and student characteristics on the skills of struggling readers. *Reading Research Quarterly, 40,* 148–182.

McCardle, P., & Chhabra, V. (2004). *The voice of evidence in reading research.* Baltimore: Paul H. Brookes.

Mehta, P. D., Foorman, B. R., Branum-Martin, L., & Taylor, W. P. (2005). Literacy as a unidimensional multilevel construct: Validation, sources of influence, and implications in a longitudinal study in grades 1 to 4. *Scientific Studies of Reading, 9*(2), 85–116.

Moats, L. C. (1994). The missing foundation in teacher education: Knowledge of the structure of spoken and written language. *Annals of Dyslexia, 44,* 81–102.

Moats, L. C. (1999). *Teaching reading is rocket science.* Washington, DC: American Federation of Teachers.

Moats, L. C. (2000). *Whole language lives on: The illusion of "balance" in reading instruction.* Washington, DC: Thomas P. Fordham Foundation.

Moats, L. C. (2004). Science, language, and imagination in the professional development of reading teachers. In P. McCardle & V. Chhabra (Eds.), *The voice of evidence in reading research* (pp. 269–287). Baltimore: Paul H. Brookes.

Moats, L. C. (2006). *Whole language high jinks: How to know when a scientifically based reading program isn't.* Washington, DC: Thomas P. Fordham Foundation.

Moats, L. C., & Farrell, L. (2007). *Teaching reading essentials.* Longmont, CO: Sopris West Educational Services.

Moats L. C., & Foorman, B. R. (2003). Measuring teachers' content knowledge of language and reading. *Annals of Dyslexia, 53,* 23–45.

Moats, L. C., & Foorman, B. R. (in press). Literacy achievement in the primary grades in high poverty schools: Lessons learned from a five-year research program. In S. Neuman (Ed.), *Literacy achievement for young children from poverty.* Baltimore: Paul H. Brookes.

National Adult Literacy Survey. (2003). Washington, DC: National Center for Education Statistics. Retrievable from http://nces.ed.gov/surveys/all/issuebrief.asp#

National Association of State Directors of Special Education (NASDSE), Inc. (2006). *Response to intervention: Policy considerations and implementation.* Alexandria, VA: Author. NASDSE Web site: www.nasde.org

National Center for Education Statistics (NCES). (2005). *National assessment of educational progress: The nation's report card.* Washington, DC: U.S. Department of Education.

National Institute of Child Health & Human Development (NICHD). (2000). Report of the National Reading Panel. *Teaching children to read: An evidence-based assessment of the scientific research literature on reading and its implications for reading instruction.* Washington, DC: National Institutes of Health. Retrieved December 5, 2007, from http://www.nationalreadingpanel.org/Publications/summary.htm

No Child Left Behind Act of 2001, PL 107-110, 115 Stat. 1425, 20 U.S.C. §§ 6301 et seq.

Olson, R. K. (2004). SSSR, environment, and genes. *Scientific Studies of Reading, 8*(2), 111–124.

Rashotte, C. A., MacPhee, K., & Torgesen, J. K. (2001). The effectiveness of a group reading instruction program with poor readers in multiple grades. *Learning Disabilities Quarterly, 24,* 119–134.

Rayner, K., Foorman, B. F., Perfetti, C. A., Pesetsky, D., & Seidenberg, M. S. (2001). How psychological science informs the teaching of reading. *Psychological Science in the Public Interest, 2*(2).

Rayner, K., Foorman, B. F., Perfetti, C. A., Pesetsky, D., & Seidenberg, M. S. (2002). How should reading be taught? *Scientific American, 286*(3), 84–91.

Rayner, K., & Pollatsek, A. (1989). *The psychology of reading.* Englewood Cliffs, NJ: Prentice-Hall.

Reading First Leadership Academy. (2002). *Blueprint for professional development* (published as a handout for participants). Washington, DC: U.S. Department of Education, Reading First Initiative.

Roberts, T., & Neal, H. (2004). Relationships among preschool English language learners' oral proficiency in English, instructional experience, and literacy development. *Contemporary Educational Psychology, 29,* 283–311.

Roehrig, A. D., Duggar, S. W., Moats, L. C., Glover, M., & Mincey, B. (in press). When teachers work to use progress monitoring data to inform literacy instruction: Identifying potential supports and challenges. *Remedial and Special Education.*

Sacks, D. (2003). *Language visible: Unraveling the mystery of the alphabet from A to Z.* New York: Broadway Books.

Savage, R. S., & Frederickson, N. (2006). Beyond phonology: What else is needed to describe the problems of below-average readers and spellers? *Journal of Learning Disabilities, 39,* 399–413.

Scarborough, H. (2001). Connecting early language and literacy to later reading (dis)abilities: Evidence, theory, and practice. In S. B. Neuman & D. K. Dickinson (Eds.), *Handbook of early literacy research* (pp. 97–110). New York: Guilford Press.

Scarborough, H. S., & Brady, S. A. (2002). Toward a common terminology for talking about speech and reading: A glossary of the 'phon' words and some related terms. *Journal of Literacy Research, 34,* 299–334.

Seidenberg, M. S., & McClelland, J. L. (1989). A distributed, developmental model of word recognition and naming. *Psychological Review, 96,* 523–568.

Shankweiler, D., Lundquist, E., Katz, L., Stuebing, K. K., Fletcher, J. M., Brady, S., et al. (1999). Comprehension and decoding: Patterns of association in children with reading difficulties. *Scientific Studies of Reading, 3,* 69–94.

Shattuck, R. (1980). *The forbidden experiment: The story of the wild boy of Aveyron.* Based on F. Truffaut (1970), *The wild child* [Motion picture]. New York: Washington Square Press.

Shaywitz, S. E. (2003). *Overcoming dyslexia: A new and complete science-based program for reading problems at any level.* New York: Alfred Knopf.

Simos, P. G., Breier, J. I., Fletcher, J. M., Foorman, B. R., Bergman, E., Fishbeck, K., et al. (2000). Brain activation profiles in dyslexic children during nonword reading: A magnetic source imaging study. *Neuroscience Reports, 290,* 61–65.

Simos, P. G., Fletcher, J. M., Bergman, E., Breier, J. I., Foorman, B. R., Castillo, E. M., et al. (2002). Dyslexia-specific brain activation profile becomes normal following successful remedial training. *Neurology, 58,* 1203–1213.

Simos, P. G., Fletcher, J. M., Sarkari, S., Billingsley-Marshall, R., Denton, C., & Papanicolaou, A. C. (2007). Intensive instruction affects brain magnetic activity associated with oral word reading in children with persistent reading disabilities. *Journal of Learning Disabilities, 40*(1), 37–48.

Snow, C., Burns, S., & Griffin, P. (1998). *Preventing reading difficulties in young children.* Washington, DC: National Academy of Sciences, National Research Council.

Snow, C., Griffin, P., & Burns, S. (2006). *Knowledge to support the teaching of reading.* San Francisco: Jossey-Bass.

Spear-Swerling, L., & Brucker, P. (2004). Preparing novice teachers to develop basic reading and spelling skills in children. *Annals of Dyslexia, 54,* 332–364.

Stahl, S. (2004). What do we know about fluency? In P. McCardle & V. Chhabra (Eds.), *The voice of evidence in reading research* (pp. 187–211). Baltimore: Paul H. Brookes.

Stanovich, K. (2001). *Progress in understanding reading.* New York: Guilford Press.

Stanovich, P. J., & Stanovich, K. E. (2003). *Using research and reason in education: How teachers can use scientifically based research to make curricular and instructional decisions.* Washington, DC: The Partnership for Reading.

Stone, A. C., Silliman, E. R., Ehren, B. J., & Apel, K. (Eds.). (2004). *Handbook of language and literacy: Development and disorders* (pp. 318–339). New York: Guilford Press.

Swanson, H. L., Hoskyn, M., & Lee, C. (1999). *Interventions for students with learning disabilities: A meta-analysis of treatment outcome.* New York: Guilford Press.

Sweet, R. W. (2004). The big picture: Where we are nationally on the reading front and how we got there. In P. McCardle & V. Chhabra (Eds.), *The voice of evidence in reading research* (pp. 13–44). Baltimore: Paul H. Brookes.

Tannenbaum, K. R., Torgesen, J. K., & Wagner, R. K. (2006). Relationships between word knowledge and reading comprehension in third-grade children. *Scientific Studies of Reading, 10*(4), 381–398.

Torgesen, J. T. (2002). The prevention of reading difficulties. *Journal of School Psychology, 40,* 7–26.

Torgesen, J. T. (2005). Remedial interventions for students with dyslexia: National goals and current accomplishments. In S. O. Richardson & J. Gilger (Eds.), *Research-based education and intervention: What we need to know* (pp. 103–123). Baltimore: International Dyslexia Association.

Torgesen, J. K., Alexander, A. W., Wagner, R. K., Rashotte, C. A., Voeller, K .K. S., & Conway, T. (2001). Intensive remedial instruction for children with severe reading disabilities: Immediate and long-term outcomes from two instructional approaches. *Journal of Learning Disabilities, 34,* 33–58.

Torgesen, J. K., Rashotte, C. A., & Alexander, A. W. (2001). Principles of fluency instruction in reading: Relationships with established empirical outcomes. In M. Wolf (Ed.), *Dyslexia, fluency, and the brain* (pp. 333–355). Baltimore: York Press.

Torgesen, J. K., Wagner, R. K., Rashotte, C. A., Rose, E., Lindamood, P., Conway, J., et al. (1999). Preventing reading failure in young children with phonological processing disabilities: Group and individual responses to instruction. *Journal of Educational Psychology, 91,* 579–594.

Treiman, R., & Bourassa, D. (2000). The development of spelling skill. *Topics in Language Disorders, 20*(3), 1–18.

Tyborowski, P., & Crosby, J. (2001). *Focus on /F/onemes: The complete phonemic awareness curriculum.* Worcester, MA: /F/onemes to Phonics.

The University of Texas. (2005). *Introduction to the 3-tier reading model* (3rd ed.). Austin: College of Education, Vaughn Gross Center for Reading and Language Arts. Retrievable from www.texasreading.org

Vaughn, S., & Linan-Thompson, S. (2003). Group size and time allotted to intervention: Effects for students with reading difficulties. In B. R. Foorman (Ed.), *Preventing and remediating reading difficulties* (pp. 299–324). New York: York Press.

Vellutino, F. R., & Scanlon, D. M. (2002). The interactive strategies approach to reading intervention. *Contemporary Educational Psychology, 27,* 573–635.

Vellutino, F. R., Tunmer, W. E., Jaccard, J. J., & Chen, R. (2007). Components of reading ability: Multivariate evidence for a convergent skills model of reading development. *Scientific Studies of Reading, 11*(1), 3–32.

White, E. B. (2005; originally published 1945). *Stuart little.* New York: HarperTrophy.

Wolf, M. & Bowers, P. G. (1999). The double-deficit hypothesis for the developmental dyslexias. *Journal of Educational Psychology, 91,* 415–438.

Woodcock, R. W., & Johnson, M. B. (1989). *Woodcock-Johnson psycho-educational battery (revised).* Allen, TX: DLM Teaching Resources.

Answer Key

Chapter 2
Learning to Read Is Not Natural

Exercise 2.1: Comparing Spoken and Written Language (p. 11)

	Spoken (Conversational) Language	Written, Academic, or Literate Language
Speech Sounds (phonology)	• Sounds are blended together in spoken words (coarticulated).	• Sounds are represented by alphabet letters. • Letters are isolated units. • Letters must be matched with sounds and sequentially processed, left to right, in space as well as time.
Vocabulary (semantics)	• Words may include incomplete or casual references. • Common words are used. • More liberties are taken with "correct" word form, such as pronouns.	• Words may be uncommon, specific to a topic, longer (especially Latinate words with prefixes, roots, and suffixes) and more precise in meaning than those used in conversation. • "Correct" word form and usage are expected.

(continued)

	Spoken (Conversational) Language	Written, Academic, or Literate Language
Sentence Structure (syntax)	• Sentences tend to be incomplete, run-on, or otherwise ungrammatical in conversational speech.	• Sentences may be lengthy, embedded (with dependent clauses), and more carefully constructed to convey specific meanings.
Paragraphs and Discourse Structure	• There are no paragraphs in spoken language. • Speech, unless written out and read, may be much more rambling, circular, repetitive, and disorganized.	• Paragraphs have a logical structure, especially in expository text. • Linking words, repeated phrases, and pronoun referents are used deliberately to make text "hang together." • Different paragraph organizations serve specific goals of logic. • Meaning must be clearly and completely put into words.
Overall Context for Use, and Feedback Available During Communication (pragmatics)	• Conversational speech is supported with gestures, facial expressions, tone of voice, and the presence of shared context or events.	• All the meaning in written language resides in the words themselves. • There is no contextual redundancy; we must imagine the author's voice and intent from our interpretation of the words.

Exercise 2.2: Simulation of Learning to Read (p. 23)

(Correct responses are given in the PowerPoint presenter's script and slides. The responses are intentionally omitted here.)

Take 2 Review (p. 27)

Knowledge/Main Ideas	Application/Details
1. Compared to speaking, which is natural, learning to read is not natural.	• Many people don't learn to read well. • For most, reading is learned through instruction and practice. • All humans have spoken a language, but only a minority have a writing system.
2. Academic, or "book," language differs from conversational, spoken language.	• Academic language is more formal. • Words are more unusual, more precise in meaning. • All meaning is carried by the words because tone of voice and body language are not present to help. • Sentences are longer, more complex.
3. English orthography is *morphophonemic*, which means that it is a "deep" alphabetic writing system organized by both letter-sound correspondences and morphology.	• English spelling often shows the meaningful parts of words, and it is not a perfectly phonetic system in which one letter represents only one sound.

Chapter 3
What the Brain Does When It Reads

Exercise 3.1: Acting Out the Brain (p. 34)
(No Answer Key.)

Exercise 3.2: The Four Processors at Work in the Classroom (p. 37)

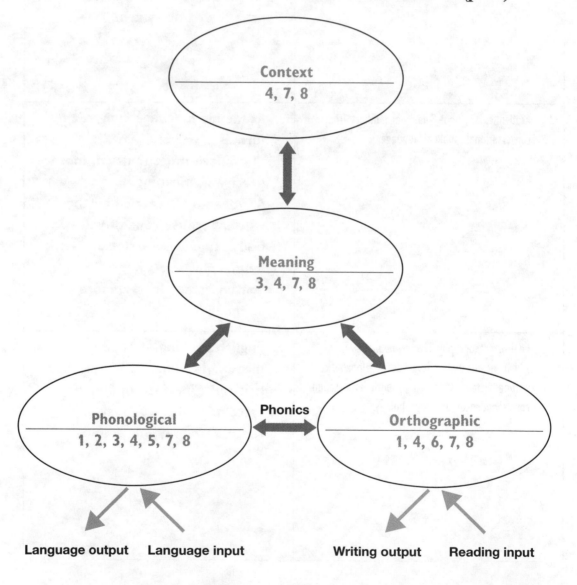

Exercise 3.2 Alternative: Processing Systems and Classroom Instruction (p. 38)
(No Answer Key. Presenter gives instructions.)

Take 2 Review (p. 40)

Knowledge/Main Ideas	Application/Details
1. Good readers process *all* the letters in printed words; they read words completely and accurately.	• Eye movement studies show that the eye of a good reader processes all of the letters; the good reader does not skip over words or guess from context. • It's not a good idea to ask students to read words by guessing from the first sound only.
2. Four processing systems must work together to support printed word recognition.	• Orthographic, phonological, meaning, and context processors each must do a special job. • Building networks between processors, or connecting the processors, is very important for good reading. • For example, ask students to apply what they have just learned in a phonics lesson to reading or spelling or writing.

Chapter 4
How Children Learn to Read and Spell

Exercise 4.1: Sounds in Letter Names (p. 49)

A   /ā/   J   /j/ /ā/   S   /ĕ/ /s/

B   /b/ /ē/   K   /k/ /ā/   T   /t/ /ē/

C   /s/ /ē/   L   /ĕ/ /l/   U   /y/ /ū/

D   /d/ /ē/   M   /ĕ/ /m/   V   /v/ /ē/

E   /ē/   N   /ĕ/ /n/   W   /d/ /ŭ/ /b/ /l/ /y/ /ū/

F   /ĕ/ /f/   O   /ō/   X   /ĕ/ /k/ /s/

G   /j/ /ē/   P   /p/ /ē/   Y   /w/ /ī/

H   /ā/ /ch/   Q   /k/ /y/ /ū/   Z   /z/ /ē/

I   /ī/   R   /ar/

Children in the early and later alphabetic stages of reading and spelling rely on letter names to derive sounds.

1. Which letter names do *not* have the sounds that the letters represent?

   h, w, x, y

2. Which letter names and sounds are likely to be most easily confused?

   c/s, g/j, w/y/u, h/ch

3. Can you think of a sound that is *not* in any letter name?

   /ă/, /ĭ/, /ŭ/, /ng/, /th/, /th/, /sh/

Exercise 4.2: Review Reading and Spelling Development With
Writing Samples (p. 55)

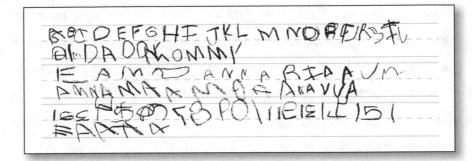

September writing sample:

This student knows many alphabet letter forms and can write her name ("Anna") and a few learned words ("Daddy," "Mommy"). However, she may not know the difference between a letter and a number, and may not understand the alphabetic principle. Even so, her knowledge of letter forms and names indicates that she is on track to become a good reader.

> a wich toock the pretty pretty princess
> ard shee brot the princess and thennti
> wich toock the priness in to the cich
> in   and the wich tide the princess
> to a char and then a prince savd
> her and then thae livd haplee evr
> aftr

April writing sample:

This student's phoneme awareness is well developed for kindergarten. Spelling is phonetically accurate, although the student has yet to develop understanding of the spelling of past tense **-ed**. This student has learned at least one major grapheme for each phoneme, such as **oo** for the sound in **took**. The use of the letter **r** for the final syllable in the word **after** is typical of students at this later stage of phonetic spelling.

Alternative Exercise 4.2: For Teachers of Older Students (p. 56)

• Read this composition that was written by a sixth-grade student, and then answer the questions below.

> "TITEL WAVE!" But befor she could do eny thing a dig hug hole opend up in the middel of the wave. The two gerles started to run, but the wave was tow fast for them. It suked them in the hole and then they startet floping around, they hit ther hedes on part of the rocy botom. They both got knoked out dead. When they woke up they were in a room whith a deap blue ceiing and the bed they were laing on was made of orol and the blanket was a dark blue tint over them. Gust then they herd the dore creek open. A girl with really long brown hair and a white sooba biving shurt and pants with a "sbc" on the shurt. Walked over to them and said "hellou" my name is Maddie, wats your name." I'm mary and shes ruby mary said. "Well come with me and lets get some food."

1. Find examples of phonetic, sound-by-sound spellings. Which of Ehri's phases best describes this trait?
   This is *later phonetic stage* spelling, in which a student represents phonemes in sequence but often without regard for conventional spelling patterns (e.g., orthography). Examples: suked, rocy, whith, wats.

2. Which processing system—phonological or orthographic—appears to be more underdeveloped in this student? Why do you think so?
   Representation of phonemes is good. However, knowledge of orthography is very poor for the student's age and grade level. For example, the student has never internalized the patterns for spelling the sound /k/: c, k, -ck.

3. This student is a dysfluent reader. Why would you expect a sixth-grade student who spells phonetically to be a dysfluent reader? (If the student moved through this stage to the next stage of reading and spelling development, what would he have to learn to do?)
   When words must be sounded out for spelling and/or for reading, they are not yet recognized or recalled automatically as "sight" words. This student should be taught about conventional phoneme-grapheme correspondences, letter sequence and syllable patterns, and spellings of meaningful parts of words.

Chapter 5
Dyslexia and Other Causes of Reading Disability

Exercise 5.1: Three Second-Grade Children With Three Kinds of Reading Problems (p. 66)

SAMPLE 1

1. Find two words in which the student left out consonant sounds.
    bump, chase, popping

2. Find two words that have digraphs (e.g., **wh**, **ch**, **sh**, **th**) but are not spelled with them.
    ship, when, chase, beaches

3. Find the word that the student spelled /v/ with the letter **f**. Why might a student confuse these two sounds?
    The word is drive; /f/ and /v/ are two phonemes that are articulated the same way except for the feature of voicing. They feel similar in the mouth, but /f/ is an unvoiced sound and /v/ is a voiced sound.

4. Find two words in which short vowels are misspelled.
    bump, when

(continued)

5. Find two words with more than one syllable. Can the student represent syllables in longer words?
    Words with more than one syllable: preparing, popping, cattle. This student
    is overwhelmed by longer words, possibly because she has not developed the
    ability to hold all the sounds of the spoken word in mind while she spells
    them.

SAMPLE 2

goo	(go)
ann	(and)
yel	(will)
hme	(him)
coc	(cook)
lot	(light)
jrs	(dress)
reh	(reach)
ntr	(enter)

1. Find the letter that this student uses for the /w/ sound. Why did she choose that letter?
    **The letter she uses for the /w/ sound is y, the letter whose name begins with
    the phoneme /w/ (i.e., y = /w/ /ī/).**

2. Find the letter she uses for the /ch/ sound. Why did she choose that letter?
    **The letter she uses for the /ch/ sound is h, the letter whose name includes the
    phoneme /ch/ (i.e., h = /ā/ /ch/).**

3. What does she think is the first sound in the word **dress**? Does that seem like a logical choice?
    **Because the /d/ in dress is changed before the sound /r/, it comes out of the
    mouth formed in a manner similar to /j/. The choice of letter is very logical.**

4. How does she spell long-vowel sounds?
    **In spelling the word go ("goo"), she writes an extra letter to indicate the
    "long" vowel. In spelling the word reach ("reh"), she uses the letter name
    that is the same as the long vowel sound.**

SAMPLE 3

> I make Baken egg Chese
> I use Chese surp Baken
> eggs . I will Bern the eggs
> I put the gres inth Pan
> then put the Baken inthepan
> I put the Beter inthe Pan
> And Chop the egg

1. What is the strength of this student's composition?

   This student intends to provide a logical and complete explanation of what to do.

2. What kinds of words are missing from the sentences?

   The conjunction and as well as helping verbs will or would.

3. Do you think he wrote fluently, or slowly and laboriously? Why?

   Sentences are short, ideas are not elaborated, and descriptive language is sparse. It gives the impression of slow, labored writing and a student who is struggling to conjure up all the words to put into his sentences.

4. Are the spellings mostly accurate phonetically? Is that a good sign?

   Yes, the spellings represent the sounds in words as the student perceives them. This is a good sign that suggests he can respond to systematic teaching.

Exercise 5.2: DIBELS and the Four Processors (p. 70)

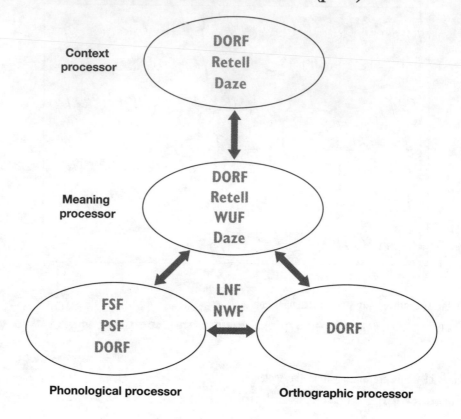

Take 2 Review (p. 71)

Knowledge/Main Ideas	Application/Details
1. Poor readers do not share the same type of reading disability; at least three subtypes are established in research.	• Phonological weakness; orthographic processing speed (fluency) weakness; language comprehension weakness.
2. A glitch in one or more processing systems may cause a reading problem.	• It's possible to have a "single deficit" or a "double deficit" (e.g., a combination of processing speed and phonological awareness difficulty).
3. The dyslexic brain may respond well to instruction.	• Successful remediation results in changes in functional brain processes and normalization of those processes.

Chapter 6
The Research Base for Understanding Reading

Exercise 6.1: Qualitative and Quantitative Research (p. 75)
(No Answer Key. Reading and discussion only.)

Exercise 6.2: Understanding Effect Size (p. 78)
(No Answer Key. Participants contribute to demonstration.)

Exercise 6.3: Shared Reading of a Research Article (p. 79)
(No Answer Key. Group shared reading and individualized grid completion.)

Exercise 6.4: Module 1 Review: Match It! (p. 81)

> **Note to presenter:** Essay answers are not provided in the Answer Key. Participants must construct their own responses from the readings and discussions. Sample responses are provided in the Presenter's Kit material.

1. Definition of *dyslexia*:   **A disorder of word reading and spelling that occurs because of weaknesses in phonological processing, in the majority of cases**

2. Most cited researcher on phases of word reading: **Linnea Ehri**

3. Percentage of oral languages that have invented a writing system: **About 10 percent have invented their own writing system. About 50 percent have now adopted a writing system.**

4. Phonological processor: **A neural network in the frontal lobe of the left half of the brain that is specialized for speech-sound perception, memory, retrieval, awareness, and pronunciation**

5. Orthographic processor: **Brain networks in the back half of the left side of the brain responsible for perceiving, storing, and retrieving letter sequences in words**

6. Semantic (Meaning) processor: Neural networks that attach meanings to words that have been heard or decoded

7. Fluency: In reading, to read with sufficient speed to support understanding

8. Double deficit: An impairment of both phonological processing and rapid automatic naming that affects speed and accuracy of word recognition

9. Undifferentiated poor reader: A poor reader who may be weak in basic reading skills and in language comprehension

10. Early Alphabetic phase: A phase of early reading and spelling development in which only a few speech sounds in each word are recognized or spelled

11. Quantitative research: Research methodology that measures and describes the relationships among variables with numbers, and that analyzes those relationships with statistics

12. NRP: The National Reading Panel of 2000, convened by Congress to do a meta-analysis of existing research on reading instruction and to make recommendations about the best ways to teach reading

13. Percentage of the adult U.S. population that cannot read well: According to the National Center for Education Statistics, 14 percent—or 20–30 million adults—in the United States are "below basic," and another 27 percent read at only a "basic" level. Thus, about 40 percent of the U.S. adult population does not read well enough to successfully summarize or interpret texts that are written at a 12th-grade level.

14. Morphophonemic: Representing both sound and meaning

15. Phonics: The study of the relationships between letters and the sounds they represent; also used as a descriptor for code-based instruction in reading (e.g., the "phonics approach" or "phonic reading").

16. Prealphabetic (Logographic) phase: The earliest stage of reading and spelling development, when letters are not used to represent speech sounds and words are not sounded out

17. Shallow orthography: An alphabetic writing system in which one letter represents one sound

Chapter 7
Leadership to Improve Reading and Language Skills

Exercise 7.1: Action Plan for Principals (p. 91)
(No Answer Key. Chart entries will vary.)

Final Review, Module 1 (p. 93)
(Answer Key is in Module 1 Presenter's Kit handouts.)

Index

Note: Page numbers in *italics* refer to the Answer Key.

A

alphabetic writing system
  advantages of, 18
  awareness of speech sounds and, 16–17
  consolidated alphabetic stage, 45, 46–47, 51, 69
  difficulty of English vs. other languages, 18
  early alphabetic reading and spelling, 45, 46–47, 48–49, 57, 69
  evolution of, 13–15, 18
  flowchart of evolution of, 15
  later alphabetic reading and spelling, 45, 46–47, 50–51, 69
  prealphabetic reading and spelling, 45, 46–48, 57, 69
  shallow and deep orthographies and, 16–17
  syllabic systems and, 14, 17
angular gyrus, 32, 33, 62
assessment
  data utilization and analysis, 85–86
  implications for, 69
  ongoing, 57
attention deficit hyperactivity disorder (ADHD), 61

B

bibliography, 119–125
brain
  Acting Out the Brain exercise, 34
  angular gyrus, 32, 33, 62
  areas involved in reading, 32–33
  context processor, 32, 33, 36–37
  developing reading brain, 42–43
  dyslexia and, 62–63
  meaning processor, 32, 33, 36
  orthographic processor, 32, 33, 35, 37, 39, 45, 46, 61, 70
  patterns, changing, 42–43
  phonological processor, 32, 33, 34–35, 39, 62
  processing systems supporting word recognition, 32–37
  reading levels and reliance on different regions of, 42
  studies of reading growth, 51–52

C

CD-ROMs, 2
Chall, Jeanne, 44–45
Colorado Teacher Preparation Program Criteria for Literacy Courses, 105–109
Connecticut Longitudinal Study, 43–44
consolidated alphabetic stage, 45, 46–47, 51, 69
context processor, 32, 33, 36–37
correlational studies, 76
cross-sectional studies, 76

D

DIBELS®, 48, 49, 70, 85, 90, *138*

discourse, 3, 10, 12

dyslexia

    ADHD and, 61

    brain and, 62–63

    defined, 59–60

    "reading impaired" definition and, 60

    related/coexisting problems, 61

    "typical" symptoms by grade level, 64–65

    uniqueness of manifestation, 63

E

early alphabetic reading and spelling, 45, 46–47, 48–49, 57, 69

effect size (ES or f), 77, 78

Ehri, model of reading progression, 45–47, 51

essential components, of comprehensive reading instruction, 31, 57–58

etymology, 3

evolution, of writing systems, 13–15, 18

exercises

    Chapter 2

        Comparing Spoken and Written Language, 11–13, *127–128*

        Simulation of Learning to Read, 19, 21, 23–26, 95–103

    Chapter 3

        Acting Out the Brain, 34

        The Four Processors at Work in the Classroom, 37–38, *130*

        Processing Systems and Classroom Instruction, 38

    Chapter 4

        Review Reading and Spelling Development With Writing Samples, 55, *133*

        Sounds in Letter Names, 50–51, *132*

        For Teachers of Older Students, 56, *134*

    Chapter 5

        DIBELS and the Four Processors, 70, *138*

        Three Second-Grade Children With Three Kinds of Reading Problems, 66–69, *135–137*

    Chapter 6

        Module 1 Review: Match It!, 81–82, *140–141*

        Qualitative and Quantitative Research, 75–77

        Shared Reading of a Research Article, 79–80

        Understanding Effect Size, 78

    Chapter 7

        Action Plan for Principals, 91–92

Extension Activities, 111–112

eye movements

    reading and, 29–30

    Warm-Up: Watch Eye Movements, 29

F

Final Review, Module 1, 93–94

fluent reading, 30, 31–32, 42–43, 45, 46, 51, 54, 69

G

glossary, 113–118

H

hypotheses, 74

L

language comprehension. *See* context processor; meaning processor

later alphabetic reading and spelling development, 45, 46–47, 50–51, 69

leadership, purpose of, 84

Learner Objectives

    Chapter 1, 5

    Chapter 2, 7

    Chapter 3, 29

    Chapter 4, 41

    Chapter 5, 59

    Chapter 6, 73

    Chapter 7, 83

LETRS modules

    chart summarizing content of, 3

    fundamental idea of, 2–3

    general overview, 1–2

    Module 1 overview, 3

    structures or systems of language in, 10

letter and letter-pattern recognition. *See* orthographic processor

logographic systems, 14, 16, 44

longitudinal studies, 76

M

meaning processor, 32, 33, 36

morphology, 3, 10

O

oral language (listening and speaking), 57, 58

orthographic processing deficit, 61

orthographic processor, 32, 33, 35, 37, 39, 45, 46, 61, 70

orthography

    LETRS modules covering, 3

    shallow and deep, 16–17

P

passage fluency, 31, 57, 58

phoneme awareness, 31, 57, 58

phonics, 31, 57, 58

phonological deficit, 61

phonological processing, 39, 45, 60–61

phonological processor, 32, 33, 34–35, 39, 62

phonology, 3, 10, 12, 106

pictograms, 13–14

pragmatics, 3, 10

prealphabetic reading and spelling development, 45, 46–48, 57, 69

processing speed/orthographic processing deficit, 61

processing systems

    DIBELS and the Four Processors, 70, *138*

    supporting word recognition, 32–37. *See also specific processor names*

    Three Cueing Systems model vs., 39–40

professional development for teachers, 89–91

Q

qualitative/quantitative methods. *See* research

R

randomized experiments, 77

reading

   brain and. *See* brain

   changing relationship between word recognition/text comprehension, 43–44

   Connecticut Longitudinal Study, 43–44

   eye movements and, 29–30

   fluent, 30, 31–32, 42–43, 45, 46, 51, 54, 69

   instruction, importance of, 6

   language, literacy and, 9–10

   myth about naturalness of, 9

   passages fluently with comprehension, 53–54

   problems, commonality of, 9

   progression, Ehri model of, 45–47, 51

   Scarborough rope model of, development, 54, 69

   skills required for proficiency, 31–32

   spelling and. *See* spelling

   as unnatural, acquired skill, 8–9, 18

   visual perception, visual-motor skills, visual-spatial reasoning and, 9

   words correct per minute (WCPM), 53

reading comprehension

   deficit, 61

   essential components of instruction, 31, 57–58

   reading passages fluently with comprehension, 53–54

   source of essential components of, 57

reading problems. *See also* dyslexia

   commonality of, 5–6

   how successful schools handle. *See* successful schools

   multiple causes of, 59

   "reading impaired" defined, 60

   related/coexisting problems, 61

   resistance to change, 84–85

   RtI and tiered instructional models, 2, 86–87

   subtypes of disability, 60–61

   types of disabilities, 61

reading stages

   described by Chall, 44–45

   essential components emphasized in, 57–58

research

   consensus based on, 78

   correlational studies, 76

   cross-sectional studies, 76

   effect size (ES or f), 77

   hypotheses, 74

   longitudinal studies, 76

   qualitative methods, 74

   quantitative methods, 74

   randomized experiments, 77

   reasons for, 73–74

   systematic, empirical methods, 74

   what it is, 74

Response to Intervention (RtI), 2, 86–87

rope model of reading development (Scarborough), 54, 69

S

Scarborough rope model of reading development, 54, 69

scientifically based classroom programs, 87–88

semantics, 3, 10

semantics processor, 39

skills, for reading proficiency, 31–32

sound-symbol associations. *See* angular gyrus

speaking

    as natural process, 8

    typical progression by age, 8

    written language vs. spoken, 10–13

speech-sound awareness. *See* phonological processing; phonological processor

spelling

    case study examples of early reading and, development, 47–51

    Chall description of reading stages and, 44–45

    Connecticut Longitudinal Study and, 43–44

    consolidated alphabetic stage, 45, 46–47, 51, 69

    developing reading brain and, 42–43

    early alphabetic reading and, 46–47, 48–49, 57, 69

    Ehri phases of word-reading development and, 45–47, 51

    later alphabetic reading and spelling development, 45, 46–47, 50–51, 69

    prealphabetic reading and, development, 46–48, 57, 69

    reading and, phases of development, 46–47

    Warm-Up: Look Closely at Spelling, 41

stages of reading. *See* reading stages

successful schools

    beyond grade 3, 89

    Colorado Teacher Preparation Program Criteria for Literacy Courses, 105–109

    data utilization and analysis, 85–86

    instruction ratios, 89

    intensive intervention, 88–89

    overcoming resistance to change, 84–85

    professional development for teachers, 89–91

    purpose of leadership in, 84

    RtI and tiered instructional models, 2, 86–87

    scientifically based classroom programs, 87–88

    summary of what they do, 83

    supplementary programs/materials, 88

    teaching older, poor readers, 89

supplementary programs/materials, 88

syllabic systems, 14, 17

syntax, 3, 10

systematic, empirical methods, 74

T

Take 2 Reviews

    Chapter 2, 27, *129*

    Chapter 3, 40, *131*

    Chapter 5, 71, *139*

teachers

    Colorado Teacher Preparation Program Criteria for Literacy Courses, 105–109

    professional development for, 89–91

Teaching Tips, 9, 39, 58

Three Cueing Systems model, 39–40
Tier 1 instructional model, 86
Tier 2 instructional model, 86, 87
Tier 3 instructional model, 86, 87

V

vision. *See* eye movements
vocabulary, 31, 57, 58

W

Warm-Ups
    Chapter 1, 5
    Chapter 2, 7
    Chapter 3, 29
    Chapter 4, 41
    Chapter 5, 59
    Chapter 6, 73
    Chapter 7, 83
    Identify a Student With Reading Difficulties, 59
    List Your Favorite Resources, 73
    Listening to Forms of Language, 7
    Look Closely at Spelling, 41
    Watch Eye Movements, 29
words correct per minute (WCPM), 53
writing. *See also* alphabetic writing system
    as acquired skill, 8
    consolidated alphabetic stage, 45, 46–47, 51, 69
    early alphabetic reading and spelling, 45, 46–47, 48–49, 57, 69
    later alphabetic reading and spelling, 45, 46–47, 50–51, 69
    prealphabetic, 45, 46–48, 57, 69
    spoken language vs. written, 10–13
    systems, evolution of, 13–15
written expression, 57, 58